FOR ME, WITH LOVE

John at the translation desk, and Elidio (centre) with his son-in-law.

For me, with love

Cameos from Armadillo Water

AUDREY TAYLOR

Drawings by David Poole

KINGSWAY PUBLICATIONS
EASTBOURNE
and
WYCLIFFE BIBLE TRANSLATORS

First published 1981

ISBN 0 86065 148 7

Scripture quotations are from the following versions, as indicated:

AV = Authorized Version (crown copyright)
TLB = The Living Bible,
© Tyndale House Publishers 1971
GNB = Good News Bible,
© American Bible Society 1976
PHILLIPS = The New Testament in Modern English,
© J. B. Phillips 1972
RSV = Revised Standard Version,
copyrighted 1946, 1952, © 1971, 1973
Division of Christian Education of the National Council of the Churches of Christ in the USA

Printed in Great Britain for
KINGSWAY PUBLICATIONS LTD
Lottbridge Drove, Eastbourne, E. Sussex BN23 6NT by
Richard Clay (The Chaucer Press) Ltd, Bungay, Suffolk.
Typesetting by Nuprint Services Ltd, Harpenden, Herts.

Contents

SOUTH AMERICA

showing Brazil and the general location of the Kaiwa Tribe

ENLARGEMENT OF THE KAIWA AREA

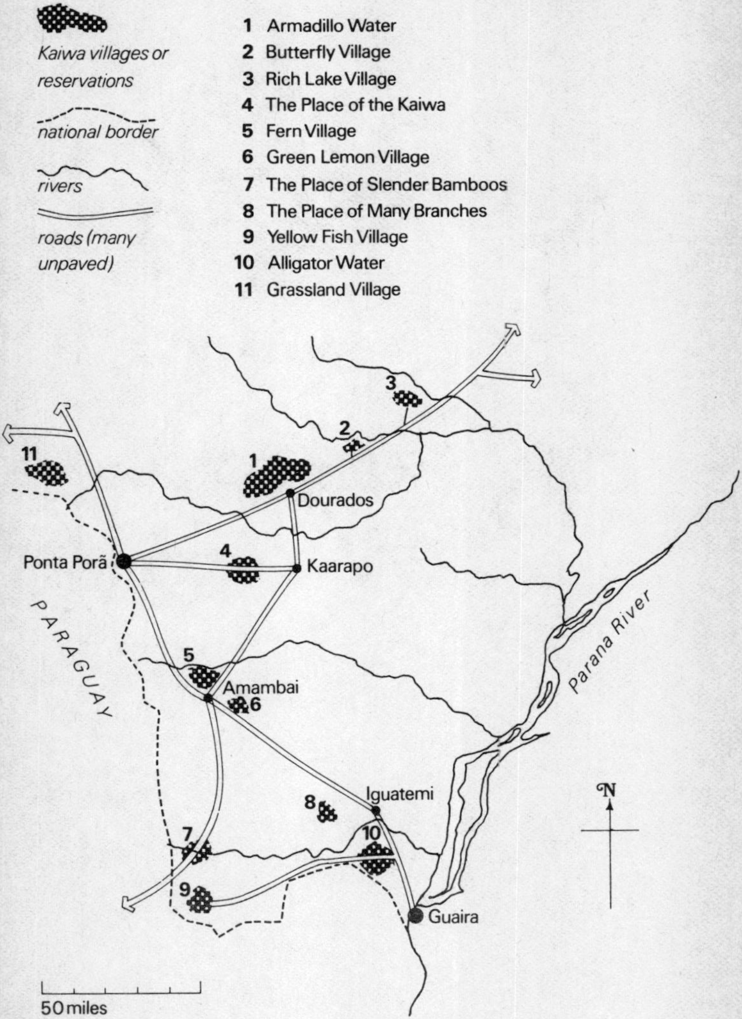

*Audrey as a child (right)
with her sister Mildred.*

Introduction

We snuggled down under the bedclothes to the music of the rain on the windowpane. For me the most exciting part of the day was about to begin. I was three and my sister was seven, and it was not uncommon in those far-off days for two little girls to share a double bed. There was something warm and comforting about it all.

After we had said our prayers and before we finally settled down for the night, we used to share a few magic moments of make-believe. My sister was the architect of those castles-in-the-air. Surely there never was a child of seven who could create, night after night, such a wealth of stories. But besides the giants and the dungeons, the fairy-castles and the impossible adventures, she sometimes threw in some real live stories just for good measure. 'What story are you going to tell me tonight?' 'Tonight . . . it will be about a little girl and a picture.' I closed my eyes so that I could imagine it all, and she began . . . .

Once upon a time there was a little girl who lived with her mummy and daddy in a nice house with a garden full of trees and flowers. She was very happy because she had just had a new baby sister, and she would often go and knock quietly on her mother's bedroom door and ask if she could see the baby. She would lean over the baby's cot and pick up her little hand and look at the tiny pink fingers as they curled tightly round her own.

"Look, Mummy, she's holding my finger," she would whisper. She really loved the baby.

One day while she was in there, she looked across the room to the shelf over the fireplace. There was never a fire in the fireplace because it was a bedroom, but there were pictures on the mantlepiece, and one of them was of a man holding a lamp in his hand and knocking at a door. (It was Holman Hunt's famous picture, *The Light of the World*.) That day she looked at the picture for a long time while she held her baby sister's hand. There were certain things about it that she didn't understand.

"Mummy," she said suddenly, "who is that, and what is he doing?" And her mummy said: "that is a very special picture. It shows Jesus, who is the Light of the World—that's why He has a lamp in His hand—and He's knocking on the door of someone's heart."

"But how is he going to get in, Mummy? There's no handle on the door."

"No, there isn't, dear. You see the handle's on the inside. That's because Jesus never pushes His way into anyone's heart. He waits for them to open it from the inside."

"Mummy, is Jesus in your heart?" the little girl asked.

"Yes He is. I opened the door a long time ago and asked Him to come in. And He did, and He's been with me ever since."

"Mummy . . . . He's not in my heart. I've never asked Him in. . . . Could I ask Him to come in now?"

So the little girl and her mother knelt beside the baby's cot and the little girl opened the door of her heart for Jesus and said: "Come in."

'. . . And do you know who that little girl was?' said my sister. 'It was *me*. And that little baby was *you*.' And she hugged me and I should have felt happy, but suddenly I felt sad, and a few tears rolled down my cheeks. She felt them, wet and unexpected on her own cheek pressed to mine.

'Why are you crying?' she said. 'Didn't you like the story? I think it's a lovely story—and it's true.'

For a few minutes I didn't know why I felt sad. After all I was only three. But the feeling I remember was that something wasn't quite right. It was a cold feeling deep inside me as of a room shut off from the sunshine. The beating of the rain on the window somehow heightened it, and I burst out: 'Jesus isn't in my heart, Mildred. I know He isn't. But I *do* want Him to come in.'

And there under the blankets with my sister's arms around me, I opened that shut door and said, 'Come in, Jesus.' And He came—I knew He had come—and it was to be for always, although I have so often through the years had to be reminded of His presence. At that moment a personal relationship began that has deepened with the years. And just as I needed to grow up from childhood to girlhood to womanhood, so I needed to grow up in Christ.

I found that being in the place God wanted me was essential to that growth, that things which make for maturity are best learned in the right setting. The setting for me was with an Indian tribe in a corner of south-west Brazil.

* * *

A cameo is a gem-stone, such as agate and particularly onyx, with carving in relief. Usually the colour-layers of the stone are utilized to give a contrasting background.

The lessons Jesus has taught me during the years I have spent with the Kaiwa tribe are like individual pictures engraved by a Master-Craftsman, with great skill and sensitivity, upon the rich background of life at *Tatu'y*, Armadillo Water.

They stand out with great clarity because they were deeply cut. Authentic cameo-carving uses the background to enhance the picture; and these experiences, carved out of my life at *Tatu'y*, have greater beauty because of their background—one which I would never have chosen myself, but which, because it was precious to Him, was hand-picked for me by the Great Artist.

This is why I have called these gems my cameos. I know I can take them out and 'wear' them again and again, as one takes out and wears a treasured brooch. To each one has been attached a gift-card, 'For you—with love.' And with gratitude I have accepted them from Him—*For me, with love.*

1

When the gods come down

It was full moon. Single-file we threaded our way along the narrow jungle path, and as we did so, the 'singing' grew louder, leading us unerringly to our destination. I smiled at my eleven-month-old son as he looked at me over my husband's shoulder. He needed reassuring as much as I did, because the sounds that were coming from the clearing ahead of us were not like anything we had ever heard before.

Suddenly we were there, immersed in a strange new world of noise, rhythm and movement. Circles of Indians, swaying and stomping to the rhythm of their song, danced—hands joined—round and round like the cogged wheels of a giant clock. The whole quite considerable clearing was a kaleidoscope of movement, if not of colour. The Kaiwa Indians had long since abandoned their own traditional clothes. The women simply put on their most respectable skirts and the men wore the least tattered of their shirts for this festal occasion. Only the witchdoctors, who boasted one or two vestiges of ceremonial dress, marked this group as distinctly Kaiwa.

Round the edge of the clearing, babies and young children, huddling in blankets, slept, cried or played unheeded.

Somebody spotted us and we were led towards the longhouse to find one of the women who was helping us learn the language. She pulled her husband from the shadows of the doorway and presented us to him. He was probably the oldest witchdoctor in the tribe. Whatever he said he was obviously welcoming us, and as he spoke to our little son, the glass-like rod that protruded from his lower lip, shone in the moonlight. Michael, too young to understand, stretched out this hand, fascinated, to grasp it. The old man moved away from what could have been a painful encounter. As he did so we noticed his headdress and wristbands of tired-looking toucan feathers

Witchdoctor in ceremonial dress.

and body-bands of tiny black seeds which covered a rough cotton poncho. These were the faded remnants of a departed glory. 'Soon "Our Father", the Great One will come,' the woman told us. 'Then you will meet him. He is the one who brings us messages from the gods.' Somebody nearby helped us to understand what was being said by translating it into Portuguese, the national language of Brazil, which we could understand. We were informed that she was referring to the most influential witchdoctor of the area. 'He will be able to see the gods when they come down and stand round the dancing floor. Then we will know what they say. Through him we will hear if they are pleased.'

The song ended with a shout and the thirsty dancers then swooped with gourd and tin-can on to the hollow logs containing sugar-cane liquor to slake their thirst. A rusty can brimming with the fermented drink was suddenly offered to us, and then as quickly whisked away and gulped down by a slightly inebriated youth. Dancers crowded round us but soon returned to the centre of the clearing to form circles of twenty or thirty people ready for the next dance.

We listened closely to the words that were being chanted over and over again, and then we asked what they meant: 'He deceived me, telling me it was afternoon.' Whatever did it mean?

'Oh, it's just part of one of our stories,' we were told.

The night wore on and still 'Our father' did not appear. The dancers got more and more rowdy as the level of the liquor in the logs went down. A few fights broke out. We were told that the party must go on until all the liquor had been drunk. In our few stumbling words we bid our host goodbye and went home to bed.

The next day we learned that when the "Great One" finally arrived, he had done so dragging his feet and lurching unsteadily. It was full day. Many of the dancers had sunk into an exhausted sleep, but those who were still awake looked at their spiritual leader and at one another in an uneasy silence.

He was drunk!—drunk on white man's liquor, and could see nothing with those unseeing eyes, much less the gods around the dancing floor. In this condition he would not hear their words. The one they trusted to transmit the messages of the gods had failed them. They helped him into a hammock.

This, then, was our first introduction to the Kaiwa Indians *en masse*—those for whom we had come 6,500 miles from the comfort-zone of our home country, to bring them the Word of Life. Living in south-west Brazil near the Paraguayan border, this tribe of nearly 10,000 Indians occupied an area about the size of Wales. In spite of years of contact with 'outsiders' (early Jesuit missionaries had lived among them three hundred years ago) they had held on to their own ways, and particularly their own language, with considerable tenacity.

After this incident I was more convinced than ever of the relevance of the Christian message. Here was a people who wanted to hear what a supernatural being had to say to them, and who recognized the need of supernatural help in their daily lives. As one Indian said: 'In these days we need someone who can help us live a good and holy life.' We had come with a message of hope, that God wanted to speak to them, and that the only mediator they needed was His Son, Jesus Christ. He would give them the power to lead a 'good and holy life'.

But they needed to hear this in their own language, because so many of them spoke virtually no Portuguese at all. They also needed to have God's Word in their mother tongue too, so that, after believing, they would grow into strong Christians.

It was obvious, therefore, that our first task was the learning of this unwritten language, and that we must also learn to live and function in this very different culture.

It had been at the invitation of a national Presbyterian mission doing evangelistic, medical and educational work among the Indians—chiefly in Portuguese—that the first Wycliffe missionaries went to the Kaiwa to work in the vernacular. They were unable to return after furlough (although latterly, after an absence from the Kaiwa of about ten years, Dr Loraine Bridgman, a member of the original Wycliffe team, has returned to the work to help bring the New Testament to final conclusion). So we were asked to carry on the work. Convinced that this was God's call to us, we obeyed, as Abraham had done so many years before: 'By faith Abraham, when he was called to go out into a place which he should after receive for an inheritance, obeyed' (Hebrews 11:8 AV).

* * *

Life among the Kaiwa was to provide me with overwhelming proof that I was not "good missionary material", but it has also provided me with undeniable proof of the Lord's unfailing love for me, shown over and over again as He has met each of my crises with a personally signed cameo.

2

Through the door

It was a hot, sultry afternoon and I was exhausted from the effort of getting my tongue round the strange sounds of the Kaiwa language which we studied for two or three hours each morning. By now I could just about manage the greeting and leave-taking replies:

. . .'*Iporã*'—It's good,' and

. . .'*Erehojevy-tama*—You're about to be going again.'

And I could ask our two language-helpers to 'sit down'. I knew words for 'bench' and 'pigeon', partly because they were so much alike, and partly because we sat on benches and watched pigeons every day with remarkable regularity.

Our small son, Michael, was obligingly taking his afternoon nap, so I stretched myself out on the hard, grass mattress, not so much with the intention of sleeping, but just to gather enough strength for the rest of the day.

I stared up at the rafters, tracing with my eye the pattern made by crossing beams and supports. Suddenly I became aware of a faint, high-pitched squeaking which seemed to be coming from somewhere among those rafters, and as it grew louder, I saw the source of the noise. A mother rat about nine inches long (not including her tail) was carrying a protesting offspring in her mouth as she made her way along the cross-beam over my head. I didn't see her return because, no doubt, she did so empty-mouthed and noiselessly, but I was startled to hear and see the same drama performed again with off-spring number two. She made the journey six times in all, and each one of the babies squeaked his disapproval of having to move house at such a tender age. By the time the sixth young rat had been transported, it dawned on me that we were housing at least seven, if not eight rats (it turned out to be twelve), and that probably we ought to take action.

It was not at all easy to rid ourselves of those extra inmates, but we made some headway in the days that followed. When it came to cockroaches, however, they were so numerous that they defied all our attempts to conquer them, and I just had to learn not to go into our kitchen area at night with a candle or flashlight, so that I wouldn't see the legions of cockroaches scattering to hide from the light.

But although I do not like rats or cockroaches, it was neither of these things that really bothered me during those first weeks of living in the Kaiwa tribe. There was something that troubled me far more deeply, something that threatened to spoil my early relationship with the Indians to whom I believed God had sent me.

In those early days, we were not living right in the Indian village. We had been loaned a disused house at the Kaiwa Mission, a few miles from the Indian reserve. Our language helpers, two Kaiwa women, came faithfully each morning and went at noon. At other times, we did not see very many Indians unless we went visiting. We knew we needed to hear the language for more than four hours a day, and we also needed to observe the culture.

Sometimes we would have what I began unconsciously to call 'nuisance visits'. I began to dread them more and more: Indians who would come with bows and arrows, necklaces or rattles, that they wanted to sell or exchange. They were mostly women, so they always wanted to see me. We had no norm by which to measure these things, and no idea of price or value. As we were to discover later, there were Indians who made a habit of exploiting newcomers like ourselves. So each time someone came, I was in turmoil. I could not judge the standard of workmanship. I didn't want to cheat them, nor did I want to be cheated. I didn't want to appear uninterested in their crafts and thus in them, nor did I want a houseful of bows and arrows.

Things reached their peak one day when a Kaiwa woman, babe in a sling, called through the open door, 'How is it?'

As I emerged, I said without too much conviction, 'It is good.' She immediately produced a diminutive bow and three small arrows, typically decorated with bamboo-strip design and dyed hen's feathers. 'Do you want your future-bow?' the lady asked. 'Take it. Look at it. It is well made.'

I took it and looked it over. Even to my unpractised eye, it was not a very high standard of workmanship.

'It is pretty . . .' I said. 'How much do you want for it?'

'I don't want money,' she told me quickly, 'I want my baby's future-clothes.'

I did not have piles of give-away clothes, but I had an attractive baby jacket, that my own baby had grown out of, so I disappeared into the bedroom and brought it out.

She rattled off a long stream of Kaiwa, which I didn't understand at all, but by various gestures I gathered she wanted more. I told her I didn't have more. Frowning, she said, 'Too little!' and was obviously not referring to the size of the garment. Then she took the bow, put it back in her sack, hitched her baby more securely on her hip, and turned and went to try her luck somewhere else. I went inside and choked back the tears of frustration.

That evening I started supper preparation as the last streaks of day were fading. John, my husband, was still outside using the last of the disappearing light to chop firewood. Michael sat in his home-made highchair (which incidentally served all our four children) and kept me company with conversational noises interspersed with his five or six recognizable words. As I stirred the soup, we carried on a kind of dialogue.

Suddenly Michael stopped his chatter and gazed beyond me to the half-open door. I turned to see who might be visiting us at that hour. The chopping still continued outside, but I could see no one at our inner door, so I said to myself, 'Oh, there's nobody there!'

As if in reply, the Lord spoke very distinctly to me:

'Yes there is,' He said. 'I'm here. Your child sensed my arrival but you didn't. I've come to you in this way because I want you to know that I am here with you—right here in this house. When Indians come I'm here to help you know what to do and give you wisdom in these difficult situations. And when you go to visit them, I'll go with you. I want you to know that you're not in this alone.'

I silently thanked Him, realizing with a sigh of relief that it was not in keeping with His nature to call me to an unknown country and then abandon me at the threshold. 'He who sent me is with me—he has not deserted me' (John 8:29 TLB). Not only was He here, but He was no stranger to all the intricacies of Kaiwa culture that at present baffled me.

Things were never the same for me after that day. I would ask Him to come to the door with me whenever visitors arrived, and He took all the tension out of those moments.

The picture of the open door stayed with me, just as His words continued to ring in my ears, and the whole experience emerged as a three-dimensional picture, unforgettably engraved on my memory. It was my first cameo, offered with His love.

3
Butterfly Village

'We're about to be going again,' said our two language helpers, Rosinha and Maria Paula.

'You're about to be going again,' I replied. By now the words tripped off my tongue effortlessly.

But the women didn't go. As they hesitated, Rosinha said, 'Are you going with us tomorrow?'

'Where to?' I asked.

'To *Panambi*—Butterfly Village,' she answered patiently. I began to suspect that she had told me about the whole thing before and I hadn't understood. So I said, 'Tell me again what's happening at Butterfly Village.'

'You know, it's the last day of the boys' lip-piercing ceremony,' she explained.

'We women are going over there early tomorrow morning, and then we'll sing and participate in the culminating festival. We want you to come with us. We're setting off at "night-finished" and should arrive when the sun's . . . there.' She raised her arm and pointed to the position in the sky she expected the sun to be, about eleven o'clock I guessed.

It would not be true to say that I understood everything she said, but I got the hang of it and said I would talk to John about it. 'It's just the women who are going, you know,' she said. 'The men have been there a week. John could meet you there.' They told me that they would leave from Rosinha's house at dawn. Then they departed, saying, 'Tomorrow we'll see you.'

Unfortunately during the night I was struck by a stomach upset of no small dimensions. By dawn I realized that I couldn't possibly make the six-hour hike along jungle trails to Butterfly Village. My inside simply was not holding together.

I was very disappointed, and as John plied me with 'binding

potions', he began to suggest other ways of getting to *Panambi*. Perhaps he could hire a *charrete*. A *charrete* is a two-wheeled horse-drawn cart with a sun canopy. The driver who agreed to take us probably had no idea what he was letting himself in for. The "road" had to be seen to be believed in places. However, both he and the horse were very patient and did their best not to jolt us too much. Michael thought it was a great experience.

We arrived at the entrance to the village just as the women were about to start their procession up to the large, central long-house, home of one of the most influential Kaiwa witch-doctors.

I clutched my stomach and told them what had hindered my joining them. They seemed to understand and told us to go on ahead to the long-house. Some of the women were still beautifying themselves with *urucu*. They would spit on their palms and rub the sticky red seeds of the *urucu* pods into the spittle. Then they smeared the paste generously on cheeks and forehead. By comparison I felt very pale.

The women arrived, singing. Then Rosinha and Maria Paula introduced us to the witchdoctor, Chikinho. He was a relative of theirs, the "Great One" we never met at the first festival.

He invited us into the long-house—a truly amazing structure. The grass roof, which reached down to the ground on all sides, was a beautiful piece of workmanship. In the dim interior, I could just make out the forms of young boys, sleeping or lazing in hammocks, their newly acquired lip-plugs protruding from ash-blackened holes in their lower lips. I counted the hammocks, twenty-six in all, and then as my eyes got accustomed to the darkness, I saw more details. Facing the eastern entrance was an 'altar' comprising several crosses in a row, each one bearing one or two gourd rattles—all important instruments in Kaiwa religion.

In each corner, cooking pots bubbled on wood fires, probably boiling up more corn to augment the supply of *kangwi* (corn liquor).

Near one fire, two women were busy completing one stage of the *kangwi*-making process, scooping corn kernels off the top of the pot, chewing and then spitting them back into the

Lip-piercing ceremony.

brew, to cause fermentation.

Near the centre of the long-house there were huge hollowed-out logs, brimming with corn liquor, which was protected from dust, dogs and children by enormous banana leaves.

Most of this I took in during the first few minutes. We were offered small benches to sit on as the women danced and chanted, pounding hollow bamboos to emphasize the rhythm of the music.

In general, onlookers were respectful and quiet as this took place. The women were in two lines facing each other on either side of the eastern entrance. They engaged in a kind of antiphonal singing which grew in volume and finally died down to almost a whisper. Michael sat on the floor quietly.

At first I thought I felt cold because the long-house was considerably cooler than outside—or was it because of my recent stomach upset? But as time went on I realized that what I was feeling was actually fear. I sensed the presence of evil in a way I had never done before in any other place. I had to remind myself over and over again that Jesus was within me, and therefore He was in that long-house.

After the women had sung, the boys in full ceremonial dress sat on their decorated benches, and the meaning and mechanics of the lip-piercing ceremony were explained to us. About a dozen boys between the ages of seven and fifteen had been chosen. After a week of instruction in tribal ways, particularly in relation to contact with the gods, they were ready for the great day. They spent the previous night in drinking and rhythmic dancing, and then as the dawn came, they were led, completely exhausted, outside the long-house, to sit in a semicircle and await the thrust of the sharpened wooden stick that would pierce their lower lips. Small glass-like lip-plugs made from clear resin were immediately inserted. From that moment they would be the "chosen ones", the messengers through whom the gods would speak to the people.

We did not stay to the end of the festivities. For one thing our driver and his horse were becoming impatient and anxious to leave.

As we made our tortuous way back, bones aching from the jolts and bumps, we asked to be released from the oppression that enveloped us. We had stepped on the Enemy's turf. Healing came to our spirits as God's Spirit touched us.

As it happened, this cameo was threaded on to a necklace of tear-drops. A few days later I lost what would have been our second child.

* * *

As far as I know, evil still holds sway in Butterfly Village. Drunkenness has increased and the people still live in terrible fear of death by knifings or witchcraft.

I dream of going back there some day, without butterflies in my stomach, but rather in the confident realization that 'greater is he that is in you, than he that is in the world' (1 John 4:4 AV).

4

Beans and pans

It actually took a whole year to get a home built closer to the Indians. Although we had had jungle training and had once built our own primitive shelter, we realized that the Kaiwa were much better equipped to build a house with local materials than we were. So we hired an Indian who was recommended to us, and gave him a rough idea of what we wanted. He apparently worked under the illusion that the longer the job took, the more he would be paid. It turned out not to be an illusion.

One thing he could never understand was why anyone who wasn't an Indian should want an Indian-style house, and we suspected that his heart wasn't really in it. Our suspicions were confirmed when, a few days after we moved in, a strong wind blew down the kitchen wall. While we waited for him to repair it, we spent several days retrieving the pan lids that blew off into the jungle beyond.

The Indians were overjoyed that we had come to live so near to them. One of the advantages of the move at this stage was that they never dreamed of talking to us in anything but Kaiwa and didn't seem to realize that we could speak Portuguese. They came to see us from far and wide, and suddenly our days became quite hectic. It was hard work fitting in concentrated language learning and simple translation of Bible stories, let alone our private devotional times. Medical work was a daily occurrence, as was a small literacy class which we started in order to check out a series of eight reading primers we had made.

Our menu was basically beans and rice embellished by locally grown vegetables and fruits. Occasionally the Indians brought us beans, but usually we bought them and the rice in bulk from the town.

One day a neighbouring Brazilian farmer visited us, and during the course of conversation asked if we would like any beans, as he had been blessed with a good crop. We thanked him profusely, and sure enough, true to this word, he came round the following day with a large sack of beans.

They say that you shouldn't look a gift-horse in the mouth, and I'm sure the saying could be adapted to a gift-sack of beans. Those beans, though delicious on the table, came to us complete with free samples of their environment. In order to get them ready for cooking, they had to be spread out and cleaned – the Portuguese expression is 'chosen'. I had to pick out every stick, stone, leaf, bad bean and bug; or conversely, I had to choose the good beans from among the rest. This was a daily chore and took longer than I care to remember. I found myself grudging the time I spent on this job and tried all sorts of shortcuts. But they all ended up causing me more work, and so I finally said, 'Well, Lord, I'm finding it hard to say "Thank you" for these beans.'

The Lord is always very patient with us, and on this occasion, I think He seemed a bit surprised at my reaction.

'But haven't you been complaining about the busyness of your days? Why, you told Me that you were having difficulty finding time to be quiet, to listen and talk to Me. Don't you see, I sent you these beans to ensure a period in each day when your hands would be doing something very necessary, but your mind and spirit could commune with Me?'

* * *

I could never have imagined myself praising the Lord for dirty beans, but that was what happened. Jesus joined me as my hands mechanically sorted the beans, and when that sack was finished, there was always something else that gave us the same kind of opportunity . . . .

But it wasn't the pans.

The story of the pans is a different one altogether, although it happened around the same time.

Besides Indian neighbours we also had some Brazilian ones —generally poor families who worked on local farms. Their houses were quite similar to Kaiwa structures, but there was one significant difference. All of them had a kitchen shelf, usually constructed of rough poles, where they displayed a row of shining pans. I learned that they got this effect with a combination of steel wool, elbow grease and time.

As these Brazilian families would also visit us from time to time (usually when no Indians were around), I began to feel a bit self-conscious about my smoke-blackened pans. So I forthwith asked John, on his next bike-trip to town, to stock up with steel wool.

Our wood-burning stove had never really functioned satisfactorily. The chimney had been built a long way from the house to lessen any danger to the grass roof, and the result was that the fire did not 'draw'. It took a long time to light and the whole thing was very frustrating. One of the most frequently breathed prayers of translator wives must surely be, 'Lord, please make this fire go.'

Even when it got going, the smoke came back in your face, and also curled its fingers lovingly all over the saucepans. Just one meal and they were all blackened again.

After John returned with the steel wool, I began my campaign for gleaming pans, and I succeeded. I felt quite proud as I gazed at them, shining like the noon-day sun. But the price was longer and longer sessions at the plastic bowl. Sometimes I wouldn't be able to visit our neighbours, which I liked to do during the sleepier hours of the afternoon, because other people would be around needing me as soon as I had finished the pan-cleaning ritual.

My Yorkshire grandmother had a saying: 'Go your own tinpot way!' It was one of her most scathing comments and usually brought you to your senses quite quickly. I'm rather glad God didn't deal with me like that, but He didn't let me go on for long. He rebuked me very tenderly:

'Audrey, when you meet Me face to face, and we take a look at your life, I won't ask why your pans didn't always shine, but I will ask you why you didn't spend more time with the Indians, getting to know them and telling them My Good News . . . .' It was enough.

And so I came to see it for what it was—my way of 'keeping up with the Joneses'. As long as the pans were clean inside, it really didn't matter what the outside was like. I would just

Audrey in her tribal-house kitchen.

have to take no notice of what people might think.

One of the results of this was a happy arrangement which became quite an institution in my life at Armadillo Water. On Saturday mornings I invited the women to come and have a pan-cleaning session with me. We all thoroughly enjoyed this, and talked and laughed together as we worked. We also extended the pan-cleaning to other kinds of cleaning and ended up having beans and rice together. Then we 'divided the spoil': those who wanted soap or needle and thread, salt or cooking fat, took home what they needed.

* * *

Although the days that followed were not without frustration and harassments, I experienced a very deep joy underlying everything we did. Sometimes I would stop and say, 'I don't remember ever being so happy,' and this contentment deepened as John and I saw the Lord touch one and then another Kaiwa life.

It had been important at that time to get my priorities straight, but I have a shrewd suspicion that these two lessons don't only apply to jungle-housekeeping.

5

Midnight music

'Yes, it's real hair!' Prascilina and her friend had both surreptitiously stroked my head as I bent over my notebook capturing in phonetic script their graphic description of how to make a hammock. I looked up and laughed: 'Yes,' I said as I held out a lock of my auburn hair, '—it's real hair, just like yours, only a different colour.'

'And curly,' they added with gestures. I didn't know the word for 'curly' so I wrote that also in my notebook in phonetics.

They were very patient with me, these two, repeating words over and over again, until I got them just right.

Prascilina was the only unmarried daughter who still lived with her parents, Basilio and Norina, our nearest neighbours. She spent many hours in our house each day, sometimes helping us to learn the language, sometimes looking at 'paper' (National Geographic magazines), sometimes playing with Michael, and sometimes just being around. It took her all of three minutes to get from her house to ours—just across the track that divided Indian land from the land where our house was built.

Her whole family took us under their wing from the very start. Basilio chopped firewood for us and planted a row of banana palms from the edge of the track right up to our house. Norina, completely unafraid of a tape recorder, grasped the microphone in her hand, and poured Kaiwa folk tales into its ever ready ear, whenever we asked her to.

It was from Norina that I learned that Kaiwa houses *could* be tidy. She swept hers daily with a broom made of the supple branches of a bush. I learned from her also that Kaiwa women *could* be materialistic in spite of their few possessions. Sometimes we think that materialism is confined to the more 'civil-

Norina, one of Audrey's neighbours.

ized' cultures. She had new saucepans hanging from her rafters which were rarely, if ever used. They were just a status symbol. And she was never more pleased than if you gave her —as payment for work or in exchange for necklaces—an item of clothing. Even if she didn't wear it, she could show it off to her friends.

Prascilina inherited this same attitude from her mother and was very concerned with possessions. Occasionally when she had money, she couldn't wait to spend it. One day she came rushing across to our house carrying something in her hand, wrapped in a piece of cloth. She looked excited as she said, 'Do you want to see what I bought?' I couldn't wait. She unwrapped the 'parcel' and presented to my astonished gaze—a complete set of false teeth, upper and lower plates. I was dumbfounded. She smiled, showing her own beautiful natural teeth, and said, 'Aren't they lovely?' She had bought them from another Indian, who had no doubt been taken in by someone wanting a bit of ready cash, and I imagine that she in turn would find a buyer when the novelty had worn off.

At the beginning of our life among the Kaiwa it was comforting to have a family close to us that really cared for us, and I appreciated the friendship of Basilio, Norina and Prascilina more than I can say. Quite early they gave us 'family' names. John was *tuty*, 'uncle', and I was *hixemirĩ*, 'younger aunt'. Michael was *ke'y*, 'older brother' and Andrew, when he arrived, became *xiryvy*, 'younger brother'. Later they were to add 'sister' and 'little-younger brother' to their extended family as Anne and Jonathan were born. They still use these names for us today.

We had a mutual caring relationship and were grateful that there were ways, meaningful in their culture, in which we could also help them. Like the time Basilio was so ill that he couldn't eat any of the food he had in his house or field. He was getting very weak, so I started making nutritious soups from all the vegetables I could lay my hands on, and taking them down to his house every afternoon, until he gained enough strength to get out of his hammock again. He never forgot that time when 'younger aunt' fed him and caused him to 'live again'.

It would be impossible to list all the things we learned from our neighbours, but certainly our knowledge of Kaiwa language and culture is richer because of them. We learned a lot about Kaiwa humour too, and it was good to be able to laugh with them about things they thought funny. That is— usually. I never could laugh with Prascilina when she pulled ants' legs off, one by one, in order to see them struggle, with less and less success of course, to run away.

But that was not the worst. One day, while looking through one of Michael's Bible story books, they came across a picture of Jesus stumbling under the cross. They asked me what was happening and after explaining in some detail, I was not at all prepared for them to roar with laughter. I remember being shocked and somehow deeply hurt. Later we were to discover that the Kaiwa have little sympathy for the weak or imperfect. Christ's falling under the weight of the cross looked like weakness to them.

Through Basilio and his family, we were also introduced to many other Indians, because their house was a kind of meeting place. When we went across the track to sit with them in the cool of the late afternoon, we would often be there when folk called, and we were accepted as part of the furniture. In this way we heard them interact with each other, and, apart from the constant slapping of legs and arms to get rid of flies and mosquitoes, those pre-sunset visits were relaxing and enjoyable and cemented our friendship with this family more and more.

* * *

One night, after we had been living in our own house for over a year, I had an unforgettable experience. . . .

Supper was over, the children sleeping, and John and I had gone out to enjoy the stars. We sat on our well and looked up into the heavens, picking out the constellations we knew—the Southern Cross, the Scorpion, Argo the Ship and Orion (upside down). We marvelled at the brightness of the Milky Way (the Indians call it the Tapir's Track). Around us the fireflies lit up the black silhouette of the jungle, like flashing lights on a Christmas tree. The still beauty of the night drew us near to God and helped us to get back our sense of proportion after a busy day.

And then, suddenly, we heard it—the monotonous drone of chanting coming from Basilio's house. They were 'singing' for the rain. Although the chanting had become familiar to us, it was particularly chilling that night. It wasn't the sound itself that made me shudder, but the fact that it stood for the power of Satan that had bound a people for so long.

These Indians were our neighbours, our friends. We had laughed and cried together, and hardly a day went by without our sharing some part of it with them. They had listened to what we had to say about God and His love, about the purpose of Christ's death, about prayer and faith, and they had said, 'We are believers. We are true believers.' Believers? Yes, they believed—in a pantheon of capricious gods who needed to be cajoled into sending rain. We knew it with sickening certainty again that night.

As we crept towards the house to listen, we heard the rhythmic shaking of rattles that accompanies the chant, and we were struck by the relentless monotony of it all, the ceaseless striving after something that is never attained. They could never be sure that they had done enough to please the spirits. We had known them go on night after night, month after month, until they were completely exhausted. How different it all was from the Christian's faith in the finished work of Christ.

We could distinguish two voices in a kind of tuneless harmony, those of Basilio and his wife, Norina. They kept up their duet far into the night, with only occasional pauses to catch their breath. By day they were 'Grandfather' and 'Grandmother' to us, but that night they seemed as far away as if a great abyss separated us. I suddenly felt the utter hopelessness of our situation, our helplessness to do anything at all against such deeply dyed beliefs as these.

But it is good to feel utterly helpless. Only then can the Lord step in and do a miracle for His glory. It is good to feel the horror of that abyss that separates us from those who dwell in darkness. Only then can our hearts be touched with an overwhelming compassion for the lost. It is good to realize that nothing *we* can do will ever bring one of these lost ones across the abyss. But, there is another truth that stands on the other side of the scale : *God* is able! He who at the dawn of time said, 'Let there be light!' is still able to cause light to shine in the darkness.

I prayed a prayer of desperation that night, but it was also a prayer of hope: 'Lord, only a miracle of Your grace can enlighten the darkened minds of Kaiwa Indians, but You are still a God of miracles. So please, Lord, *You* touch them and by Your Spirit turn them to the Truth.'

6

Snakebite

There are at least two ways of catching armadillos, and residents of *Tatu'y* used both. Basilio's method took days to make. It was a deadfall trap, which he set in a quiet part of the jungle behind his house, leaving it so delicately sprung that sometimes a sudden gust of wind would cause it to go off. It didn't only catch armadillos, but other kinds of small game would wander unawares into it, and find their way into Norina's stewpot.

The other method was less work, but involved going out during the night and waiting long hours beside the armadillo's track to the waterhole, in the hope of seizing it as it went down to get a drink.

Armadillo meat is considered such a delicacy, however, that the long vigil is worth the effort.

* * *

'Mba'eixapa?' 'How are things?' We heard the call as we were swallowing breakfast and John went to see who had come. There seemed to be a note of urgency in the man's voice.

After the barest minimum in the way of preliminaries, he blurted out:

'A man has been bitten by a snake!'

We asked, 'Who? When? Where?' and quickly pieced the story together.

It seemed that Elidio, one of the young Kaiwa we had come to know recently, had been out the previous night with his brother, hunting armadillo. His long wait by the animal's track was rewarded as he saw it scuttle past him in the moonlight. Quick as a flash he had both hands on its tail and even though it wriggled and strained, trying to free itself, he didn't let go.

But this particular armadillo was not going to give in so easily, and seeing a hole in a nearby tree stump, he headed for it, only to find that it was already occupied! The sleeping snake, a deadly *jararaca*, annoyed by the disturbance, bit deep into the two hands that still held the tail. Elidio's yelp of pain brought his brother to the scene. He killed the snake and then, carrying its still-writhing body, he helped his brother back home.

Elidio, trying to catch an armadillo, is bitten by a snake.

As far as we were able to calculate, this had happened at least four hours before. We knew that a *jararaca* can kill a man in eight hours flat, so we prayed desperately for wisdom.

I had mentally pinned over my medicine shelf the following maxim: 'Remember you are a personal friend of the great Physician,' and I had needed to consult Him on many occasions, but never so urgently as today. He showed me immediately that my own medical resources were quite inadequate for such a crisis. John and I were both convinced that we should try to get Elidio to the Kaiwa Mission Hospital as soon as possible.

John jumped on his bicycle and contacted a Christian farmer, who immediately dropped the work he was doing in his fields to prepare his *charrete*. Meanwhile John went to the sick man's house to devise a way of bringing him to the track that ran past our house. It proved to be no easy matter.

As John approached Elidio's house he could hear someone chanting and shaking rattles in an attempt to ward off approaching death.

Elidio was lying on his bamboo-pole bed, so bloated by the poison that he was unable to sit up. The entrails of the snake had been wrapped around his chest in the hope that they would 'draw the poison out'. In spite of these precautions, Elidio's wife, Julia, could see her husband rapidly slipping away. John saw that there was no time to lose.

He asked for a hammock, thinking that it would, perhaps, be easier for two of them to carry Elidio that way. But Julia didn't have one and no one seemed willing to lend one. Someone said: 'What's the use? He's going to die anyway.' John realized than that the only thing to do was for him to carry Elidio out.

It was a slow procession that moved along the narrow jungle trail. John carried Elidio piggyback style, but had to stop every few yards to let him rest, as the pain was so intense. At one point Julia pleaded with John to take her husband back home and bring medicine to him, but everyone knew that this would be fatal and encouraged them to go on. At one point the track led across a stream. The bridge was a narrow tree trunk. After that hurdle there was still another half-mile to go uphill towards the road. The sun beat down mercilessly on the small group as they struggled up to the place where the *charrete* was waiting. By this time Elidio's eyes had already turned up so that only the whites were showing. The situation looked quite hopeless. At best it would take another hour for the old horse to reach the hospital even if he hurried.

Julia climbed up to sit beside her husband and as the *charrete* moved off, John gathered the little group of Indians together (Basilio was one of them), and prayed in Kaiwa that God would make Elidio live. It was a prayer of faith in more ways than one. Not only was it the first time that John had ever prayed in Kaiwa, but it was also beyond all human expectation that Elidio should recover.

Back home, it was proving to be a long day. We waited until dusk for the first news, punctuating the hours with impromptu prayers usually instigated by Michael, who had obviously been impressed by what had happened.

It appeared that Elidio was in a coma long before he arrived at the Mission hospital. Seeing his desperate state, the hospital staff had dropped everything else to attend to him.

It 'happened' that the doctor, who visits only once a day, was there when Elidio arrived. He sent someone off immediately for the only medicine which he believed would help Elidio at this stage.

Although the nearby town of Dourados was thoroughly combed, not one chemist had the medicine in stock, and the jeep returned empty, except for some packages that had been picked up at the Post Office.

Loide Andrade, besides being one of the directors of the Kaiwa Mission, was also the architect of its hospital. An experienced nurse herself, she was used to battling for Indians' lives, both medically and spiritually. She called all the hospital staff together and they prayed; prayed for Elidio, and for wisdom for themselves—and prayed for the needed medicine.

It was then that Loide remembered the packages. She looked them over and saw that they had been sent from Rio by a well-known pharmaceutical company. They contained free samples of a wide range of medicines . . . and in the bottom of the last parcel, there *it* was!

Elidio was in and out of a coma for four days and Julia stayed right beside him. Only on the fifth day was he considered to be out of danger. Slowly we let out our breath.

After Elidio returned home, weak but rejoicing, he was a frequent visitor to our house. He bore in his hands the undeniable marks of his near escape from death, and does so to this day. Whenever he shakes hands with me I'm reminded of it again.

But he was in no doubt as to who had saved his life: 'Jesus, the One John teaches about, it was He who made me "live again",' he would say.

By this time the translation of Mark's Gospel was almost finished. We would read it whenever possible, to small groups or individuals, in our home or theirs.

Elidio loved to listen, and one day, leaning over the paper as John read to him, he said eagerly: 'I too want to read the words of Jesus. I want to learn more about Him.'

With deep thanksgiving I realized that God had honoured that first halting Kaiwa prayer, offered in faith, and had demonstrated His power in a way that left a lasting, and in some cases eternal impression on the Indians who lived at Armadillo Water.

7

A bottle of honey

When Chikinho's daughter visited me from Butterfly Village, she brought me a present. As she handed me a sack containing several *tumbyky*, small marrow-like squash, I told her regretfully that my house was full of *tumbyky*.

During the previous week I had exchanged *tumbyky* for salt, soap, oil, rice, milk-powder and money respectively, and I saw no hope of our family's consuming yet more squash. They didn't like it anyway.

But when she said it was a present, what could I do but receive it? I was touched by this act of kindness because it was rare.

Quite early in our experience with the Kaiwa we had learned to say, 'About-what are you bringing this?' when presented with bananas, sweet-corn, manioc, squash or whatever. This meant, 'What do you want in exchange for it.' Occasionally I had received the answer *'Mba'eve,'* which at that time I thought meant 'Nothing', and I would think: 'This, at last, is a true gift, given for the love of giving.' But I sensed a disappointment on those occasions when I returned the empty sack and said how happy I was (their way of saying thank you). Later I discovered, to my acute embarrassment, that in certain linguistic situations *mba'eve* can mean 'anything'. Those particular Indians were saying in effect: 'Oh, give me anything you like in exchange.'

So here I was now, actually receiving a present. She used the Portuguese word *presente* in the middle of the Kaiwa sentence, so that I couldn't possibly misunderstand.

I took the sack of squash and deposited the contents on my already considerable pile, folded the sack and took it back to her, and told her how happy I was.

She took the sack and looked at it with a puzzled expression. It was obviously empty. To make quite sure, she opened it up and peered inside. As her head emerged she said: 'But where's *my* present?'

In Kaiwa thinking there are two things that are considered to be the worst sins—to be angry and to be stingy. We had to be very careful about the way we corrected our children, as a sharp word could be interpreted as anger. As for stinginess, I'm afraid I must have appeared very stingy on the occasions when I unconsciously misinterpreted the culture.

On the whole we tried to give people what they asked for and would also give for the love of giving, but we were aware of the danger of becoming only the bearers of material good, and not fulfilling our calling to be bearers of spiritual blessing.

It was incidentally through one of those moments of spontaneous giving that we discovered the way the Kaiwa express 'grace'. I had given a woman a pan with a lid because she had told me she needed one and that she didn't have money to buy one. Later John heard her say: 'Audrey really knew how to look at me.' He was puzzled by the expression and made a mental note of it. When he enquired of his language helper what this meant, describing the situation, he was told: 'O yes, Audrey really knew how to look at that woman. She *saw* that the woman had a need and didn't have money for it, so she gave the woman what she needed without asking for anything in return.'

So here was a way of expressing 'grace', the giving of something to someone whose only condition is need. Neither merit nor money is required, and that is all that God asks of us.

But I was still puzzled. I still did not know how I could recognize a gift given to *me* just for the love of giving. So one day I prayed: 'Lord, if the Kaiwa do have a way of giving a gift without any strings attached, I'd really like to know what it is.'

* * *

One afternoon, when the house was comfortably full of Indians, I saw Julia coming up the path with her two small daughters. She greeted me and sat down along with the others, took a National Geographic Magazine from the table and soon became engrossed in it. Occasionally she would point things out to her children, or ask me what a certain picture was, but she did not appear to be in a hurry and when I asked her if she had come for medicine, she said no, they were all well.

Gradually the group dwindled as one and another said: 'I'm about to be going again.' Some had come with medical needs and others just to visit, and we all sat around companionably, talking of this and that.

Finally I noticed that Julia and her two little girls were the only ones left, and when she saw that the last person to leave was well out of earshot, she took the sack that she had pushed behind her feet and opened it. Then she drew out a bottle of golden honey and held it out to me: 'Would you like some honey?' she said.

It was pure honey. Elidio had seen bees swarming high in a tree, and had felled the tree, risking the stings, in order to get this prize. And here was one of the litres. I knew it could be sold for a good price.

I said: 'It looks really delicious honey, Julia. About-what did you bring it?'

'I didn't bring it about anything,' she said, 'I brought it for your children.'

It was as though a light went on in my head, and as I told her how happy I was, she didn't realize just how happy. As I thanked her, I silently thanked the Lord too, for showing me so beautifully what I needed to know.

* * *

Since then there have been many occasions when Indians have brought things 'for our children'. What I learned that day has been confirmed over and over again.

The cameo that emerged, however, had a touch of alabaster about it. It went beyond Kaiwa culture to a spiritual principle. A true love-gift to Christ will bring blessing to His children, just as the fragrance of Mary's love-gift perfumed the whole house.

8

Frostbite

All our four children started walking at the age of nine or ten months. I was very grateful for this as it meant that they spent less time crawling in the red dirt, and it was certainly easier on the washing. But in the process of learning to walk they had the usual number of tumbles. They simply got up and tried again, and occasionally suffered a grazed nose and a few tears. It was to be expected.

Why, then, did I not expect Kaiwa 'babes', new in the faith, to fall sometimes as they learned to walk; they who as yet had so little of the 'milk of the Word' to grow strong by? They fell, it seemed at one time, quite frequently, and I always got very depressed about it.

One of the greatest scourges of Indian life is the availability of cheap liquor. It has ruined many Kaiwa families and sometimes causes suicides. Although the women are by no means immune, it is particularly a problem for the men, especially when they go to work on Brazilian farms for a month at a time. They often spend their meagre earnings on *pinga*, cheap gin, and fill their otherwise empty evenings with drinking. It seemed that most of the Indians around us were affected; there was a lot of poverty and unnecessary misery.

Elidio and Julia had taken a definite stand as Christians, and had been baptized at the Kaiwa Mission. Sometimes this kind of thing caused jealousy, and in any case, Armadillo Water was like any other village for gossip. So when rumours filtered through to us that Elidio was drinking we wondered whether there was any truth in them. We ourselves never saw him drunk, but all doubt was removed when one of our trusted Brazilian neighbours told us that he really seemed to have a problem.

We noticed that he visited us less and less, and Julia would always be saying: 'Oh, Elidio was going to come and see you today but he's got a terrible headache,' or, 'He had to go and see so-and-so today; tomorrow he'll come.' But he never came. It weighed on me heavily.

One Sunday morning as we were going across the field to attend a small meeting of Brazilian Christians, we met a drunken Indian, bottle in hand, hardly able to sit on his horse. We knew he had recently been cured of tuberculosis at the Mission Hospital, and that his father was the 'captain' of the neighbouring village of Bororo, and a Christian. It just seemed as though all the love and care that had been lavished on him had been wasted.

We had not been sitting in the little church long when there was a terrific hullabaloo outside. Another Indian, completely drunk, was jumping about, brandishing a knife and shouting. Through the window I saw that it was Prascilina's husband, and my eyes filled with tears. The whole of the once-peaceful Armadillo Water seemed now to be dominated by alcohol.

I came out of the church by myself and started back across the field for home; and it was just as if the jungle around me reverberated with laughter. It wasn't the drunken laughter of Indians wending their unsteady way home; it was satanic laughter, and he seemed to be saying: 'A little while ago I had these people in my grip because they were devoted to their old religion, their rattle-shaking and chanting. Many of them don't bother about that any more. But I've got them in the grip of something stronger now, and it's spreading its tentacles into every Kaiwa home.' It was so real I felt I could hear him laughing, claiming that God was powerless to accomplish anything in that place.

Suddenly I stood stock still in the middle of the field and I looked up and said, out loud, 'Lord, please do something to show that You are more powerful than he is.'

But Satan scoffed at me, saying: 'Look at Elidio. You hoped for great things from him, didn't you? But I've got him too.' So I cried: 'Lord, send Elidio back to us.'

The next day was the day I had asked several women, including Julia, to come for their first reading class. We had a good time and at the end I told them that John was willing to teach their husbands to read too.

'When shall I tell Elidio to come?' Julia asked John.

'Tell him to come tomorrow and we'll fix something up,' he said.

He arrived almost before we were up the next morning and told John: 'I really do want to learn to read. I'll come tomorrow and I'll bring my brothers.'

The next day dawned black and glowering. The men had to come quite a distance, and all Kaiwa Indians are reluctant to be out in the rain. John echoed my thoughts when he said: 'Well, I'm afraid they won't come this morning.' But our faith was too small. All three brothers arrived, and a new chapter began. They came regularly and made slow but steady progress in both reading and writing.

Sometimes they stayed all day and helped John with translation or worked on a nearby farm, while I was involved with the women's class. On those days we gave them a substantial lunch. One day John was called away at lunch time to take a sick Indian to the Kaiwa Mission Hospital. I served lunch to the three men and as I retired to the kitchen, I heard Elidio say, 'John isn't here today, so I'll pray. "Lord, I really believe in You. It is You who has given us this food, and You are the One who takes care of us. You sent your Son to die for us and I want You to know that I love You." '

Towards the end of that tribal session, we said one day: 'We'll come and visit you on Sunday.' Immediately they said: 'Won't you have a meeting with us? Can't we sing? Can't we read and pray?'

They invited a few of their neighbours and relatives to join them. The Indians themselves led the service, praying and choosing their own hymns. As none of them were yet fluent readers they asked John to read a passage from Mark's Gospel.

Later Elidio said to the others: 'In the old days we were told by our fathers that there were gods who spoke to us. But those old gods don't speak to us any more. We need somebody who can help us live a good and holy life. It is only the true God, who sent His Son Jesus that speaks to us today. That's why we have confidence in Him.'

Elidio's problems were not all over. Even though he grew stronger in those days, there were more temptations ahead that he didn't resist. I remember once praying: 'Lord, did You save him from death by snakebite just for this kind of life? He's weak; he falls into one temptation after another. Is he truly Your child?'

Perhaps it was no coincidence that the banana palms outside our house were struck by frost. Just as they were unfurling those beautiful green sheaths, the frost came. In one night they were finished—blackened, lifeless. Our Brazilian neighbour came and quickly cut off all the dead, black leaves. The palms were pathetic now, just stumps three or four feet high, like so many tombstones. But within less than a week they were unfurling new green leaves again, undaunted by past frosts or the threat of those to come.

Those banana palms became a parable to me. Where there is true life it is never destroyed. 'We may be knocked down but we are never knocked out' (2 Corinthians 4:9 PHILLIPS). And this is true for our Kaiwa brothers also.

* * *

It is interesting that God used John and another Kaiwa to help Elidio overcome his drinking problem. The first step was to admit that it was a problem, and this admission grew out of an experience Elidio and John had together.

It was the end of the dry season and many of the neighbouring farmers were preparing for planting by burning off their fields. This is always of paramount danger to grass-roofed houses, and our house was therefore in a very vulnerable position. The general idea is to burn off a field on a still, windless day, so that sparks will not be carried far and wide to descend on unsuspecting roofs. However, you can't always be sure that a strong wind won't suddenly sneak up on you.

John received word that the field behind our house was due to be burned off at two o'clock one afternoon. Elidio and Avelino, another Christian Kaiwa, arrived to help John in case there was any trouble. The house was also full of numerous women and children. I was not at home.

It was a hot afternoon, and soon after the burning started, a wind got up. When the Indians saw what was happening, they realized that the house was in great danger and immediately offered their advice—lots of it. But it was Elidio and Avelino who saved the house that day. Besides helping to take all the furniture and goods out, they tirelessly soaked the grass roof with water for the duration of the burning, even though the heat was intense.

When it was over, John thanked all those who had helped, but felt especially indebted to Elidio and Avelino. This did something for Elidio. Because he had been able to help John in a particularly difficult situation, John noticed that they were able to talk to each other more as equals than ever before. This gave Elidio the confidence to talk to John about his drinking problem and ask for special prayer.

Martin Aquino was the Indian whose testimony made a profound effect on Elidio at this time, and helped him overcome this particular temptation. He, unlike John, had been through the same experience as Elidio, and had emerged victorious.

The first time I met Martin outside his own simple home at *Taquapiri* near Fern Village, we sat on a log and talked about Jesus. I have rarely met such a gentle, radiant person. It was hard to believe that before he had become a Christian, he had been a wild drunken killer. After one brawl his enemies hadn't bothered to give him that final stab because they thought that he was dead already.

'But,' said Martin, 'God saved me from death that day because He wanted to save me from eternal death, and send me to my own Kaiwa people to tell them that He loves them too.'

Martin's testimony, including his experience in overcoming drink, was so beautiful that we asked him to record it, so that Kaiwa who lived in other villages could hear it too.

He willingly did this, and so it happened that Elidio was able to hear Martin recount his experience. He listened with rapt attention and asked for the tape to be played again. Here was someone who spoke his language perfectly, who understood his problem from personal experience, and who had overcome it through the power of the Spirit of Jesus.

Elidio learned to claim this same victory at the moments when his old associates came to him: 'Let's go down to the *bolicho* for a drink. Come on, Elidio!' With God-given resolution and without hesitation he would reply—'No!'

Martin, a Christian Kaiwa, preaching to his own people.

9

Give me a banana . . .

There were some days when we would wake to hear the rain drumming on the roof (and sometimes feel it coming through) and then we knew it would be a different sort of day. Sometimes the day would start dry but with a heavy sky full of ominous clouds. The effect on people's movements was the same. They stayed where they were.

Nobody minded the rain, except perhaps mothers who couldn't get the washing dry. Most people were glad when it rained because of the crops and because it brought the temperature down a few degrees.

After a few days of rain there was the problem of getting around, and you only went somewhere if you had to. Walking in shoes was impossible. At each step you added another layer of heavy mud, and after about ten paces, your foot simply left your shoe behind. It was much easier barefoot, but dangerous because of the risk of infection, and so s-l-o-w!

If you tried to go by bicycle it was worse yet. After twenty yards or so, the wheels would become jammed with mud and slither to a sticky halt. Indian men probably had the best solution. They made 'shoes' from sections of car tyres and laced them firmly on to their feet with strips of cloth. They also used this type of protective footwear when they worked in their fields.

We didn't expect Indians on rainy days. We used the time to catch up on all kinds of neglected jobs, particularly organizing and typing up the Scripture passages currently being translated. As the rain got heavier, we would need to place tin cans in strategic positions, and move the furniture around a bit.

On one such day when the sky obviously promised a generous downpour, I had just settled the children to their first lesson and was throwing out the water from my plastic washing-up bowl, when I heard the sound of voices. A group of Indians, two women and some children, were going past our house along the track that eventually leads to the nearby town. The two women carried sacks containing what was probably beans, and I wondered for a minute if they had ever looked up at the sky. It was very unusual for anyone to make the two-and-a-half-hour trek to the town on such a day as this, unless it was a matter of life or death.

Having a town so close to an Indian reservation is a mixed blessing, if it's a blessing at all. Some Kaiwa spend a lot of time going there to 'try their luck' at making money. The results are depressing. Many have spent what they earn before they leave the town and stagger home with the usual excuses.

John was on the front verandah when this little group passed, and after greeting them he said, pointedly:

'It's going to rain.'

'Perhaps it will rain, and perhaps it won't,' they replied and went on.

About fifteen minutes later, the first few drops fell, so we were not surprised to see some of them come running past us again on their way back home. But the younger woman was not among them. She had apparently decided to go on anyway and, because a woman never travels alone, she had taken a child, probably her sister, for company.

It rained solidly all day until about four o'clock. From time to time we would say to each other: 'That girl is going to get very wet. Fancy risking a five-hour trek to town and back on a day like this!'

By the time the rain had stopped we were, ironically, out of water, having already used what we had caught from the roof. Our well had dried up several months before. Everybody, except me, went off to get water from our neighbour's well, each child carrying an appropriately sized container.

While they were gone I busied myself with the fire and started to think about supper. As it was still wet and cool, I had the side door closed but the kitchen shutter was open.

'*Mba'eixapa?* How are things?'

I was startled by the voice and looked over to the open window. The girl was there by herself. She had left the child on the track guarding the sack. Her wet clothes clung to her body and

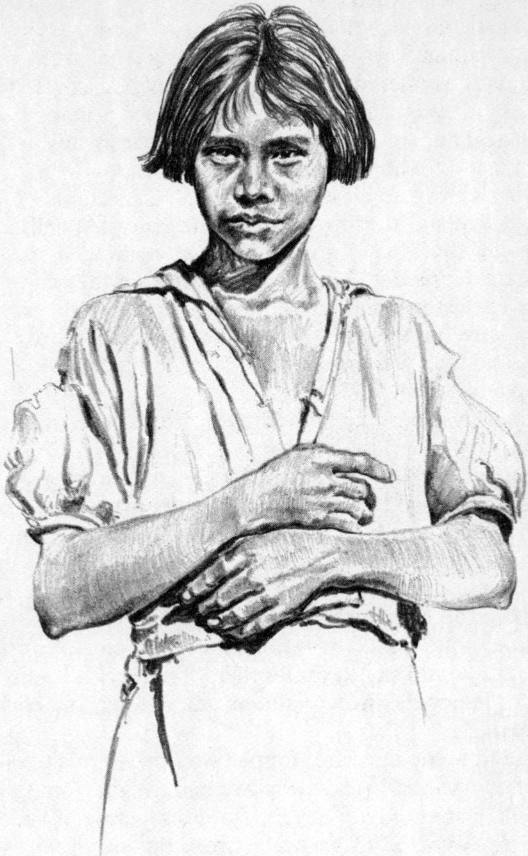

Kaiwa girl.

her hair hung lank and dripping. I suppose she was about eighteen.

'I'm all wet,' she said, 'and cold.'

I wanted to say: 'I'm not surprised. What do you expect if you go off to town on a day like this?' But instead I said: 'Yes, you are wet. Why don't you hurry home and dry your clothes?' Her home was not far away.

'I'm very hungry,' she said next. 'I haven't eaten anything all day.'

I thought: 'Well, why did you go in the first place? You should have stayed at home by your fire, and then you would have been dry and had food to eat.' But I said: 'Our food isn't cooked yet.'

'You have some bananas over there,' she said, pointing with her chin to a bunch on top of the cupboard. 'Give me a banana . . . .' She spoke peremptorily and it annoyed me, but I broke off a couple and handed them to her. She took them, threw the skins over her shoulder, and then without the usual leave-taking courtesy, she was gone. I watched her join her sister, and saw them go slowly up the track and out of sight.

Suddenly I felt ashamed. I had given her a banana with my hand, but I had not given her a banana with my heart. And she knew it. My reactions had been governed by the irritation I felt, not by the love of Christ. Tears stung the backs of my eyes. A disturbing thought was formulating in my mind, and finally it confronted me:

'It could be that all she will ever know of Jesus is what she saw of Him in you today.'

She never came back.

10

A piece of blue cloth

Whenever we came back after a month or two out of the tribe, we always spent the first few days catching up on the news.

People would drop in at all hours of the day to say 'Welcome back', and tell us their version of local happenings. Sometimes they would say: 'I want to "encase my words in your word-container" [tape recorder],' particularly if they had a dramatic event to recount.

I remember one occasion when the general gossip, coupled with these recordings, added up to a pretty depressing picture. We heard about drunkenness, knifings and violence with such regularity that, even allowing for exaggeration, we knew it couldn't all be rumour. We met sad families where the father had died in a drunken brawl, or where the daughter had been abandoned by her young husband. I was crushed when I heard that a young seventeen-year old girl, whom we knew well, had committed suicide just after her second child was born.

During the last months of pregnancy, Hortensia had been almost unable to walk because her husband, constantly drunk, had beaten her so much. Then he had gone off with another girl. He was her second husband. There wasn't much to choose between him and the first, who had abandoned her before her first baby was born.

She became so depressed about her health and about the prospect of another mouth to feed, that she told her family that she would kill the baby as soon as it was born. But they had persuaded her to go to hospital, where she was lovingly cared for until the baby's birth. She returned to her parents' home with her baby, much improved in health, but still unable to shake off the depression.

One day she picked up a piece of soap and said to her sister that she was going to the water-hole to take a bath. Her baby was sleeping in a tiny hammock and her first-born was toddling around with his uncle and aunts who were only a little bit older than he was.

She didn't return as quickly as usual, so her sister, wondering why she was delaying, went off down the narrow trail to find out. As she rounded the first bend, she saw a pair of shoes, Hortensia's shoes, placed tidily side by side in the middle of the track. She thought it was a strange place to leave them, but she was not prepared for the sight that met her eyes round the next bend. Hortensia was hanging from a tree, for ever beyond hearing the scream that involuntarily escaped from her sister's lips. The 'rope' round her neck was a strip of cloth torn from the bottom of her skirt.

'Lord, I can't take this,' I said.

By contrast, news from Kaiwa villages further south was full of encouragement. Churches were flourishing and believers were sending messages to us pleading for more Scriptures. They urged us to move down south and continue translation work there. It all sounded very tempting.

Some American friends of ours came to see us for a few days during this time, and we spent some of the time visiting Kaiwa homes in the area and introducing our friends to them.

We went one day to Maria Joana's house and, while chatting with her, admired her beautifully constructed *oypy'sy*, an old-style Kaiwa house with a grass roof reaching down to the ground on all sides. Neighbours quickly gathered round and some appeared with bows and arrows, necklaces and rattles for the benefit of our friends.

While this was going on I noticed a young couple approaching, carrying a naked child about four years old.

'Can you do something for our little girl? they said. 'She was scalded with boiling water.' I didn't stop to ask questions then, but later discovered that the parents had gone to town, leaving the older sister, a girl of about eleven, in charge of the house and family. Apparently, as the day wore on, she had become exasperated with her little sister, and in a moment of desperation, had thrown a pan of boiling manioc water over her.

There was no doubt that the burns were serious and that the child was in pain. She couldn't bear to be touched and screamed every time her mother moved her. She was also incredibly dirty. I had not set out that day armed with medical supplies, and so was not able to give any immediate help, but we reminded the parents that the Kaiwa Mission Hospital was not far away, and asked why they hadn't taken the child there. They made various excuses which we knew did not reflect the real reason, and as we went sadly away we wondered why it was so easy for the Kaiwa to believe lying rumours, and so difficult for them to believe the truth. Rumours such as: 'When they "stab" you at the hospital [give you an injection], they are really putting poison into you,' and 'If you go there you'll surely die,' were frequently spread around.

On our way back that evening I knew we would pass close to the little girl's house. During the day I had not been able to forget her, and so I acquired some dressings and we stopped our vehicle as near to her house as we could get. It was already dark.

John went along the narrow trail to tell them to bring the child to us, so that we could use the lights of the car to see by. It was very difficult cleaning away the dirt and dressing the burns, which were extensive, especially as the only place we had to lay her was on the seat of the car. Every movement was painful to her and she cried most of the time, but somehow the task was done. The parents were touchingly grateful and promised to bring her back to us so that the dressings could be changed and we could keep an eye on her.

The days passed and she did not reappear. I suppose it wasn't surprising, but I was disappointed. And then, one day, John passed the child's father on his way back from the town. He screeched to a halt and leaned out of the Land Rover to ask about the little girl.

'She's better,' he said. 'She's almost well.' Which, being interpreted, means: 'She hasn't died yet.'

'Why haven't you brought her to our house as you promised?' John asked.

'Oh well, I haven't had time,' he said. 'Tomorrow I'll bring her.'

John wasn't taking any chances, so he said: 'Why don't we go and get her now?'

When John arrived with them, our house was full of other Kaiwa, who looked on fascinated as I cleaned the child up and renewed the dressings.

All the other Indians wanted to know how it had happened, and I suppose it was then that I discovered the full story.

Finally the man left, carrying his little daughter and promising to come back 'when it is another dawn'—a promise which he again failed to keep.

As he disappeared round the bend in the road, the group of Indians who had stood up to watch him go all began to talk at once. What they said was a tragic comment on the current situation.

'That couple have stopped planting,' they told us. 'They spend their time going to the town. They leave their children alone, almost every day, and go to the town.'

'Why do they keep on going to the town?' I asked, baffled. 'Do they go there to sell bows and arrows?'

'Oh no, they go round the dustbins to see what they can find. They usually find enough food thrown out, to keep themselves from getting hungry. They bring some of it back for the children. That's how they live. Sometimes they find other things too.'

'Do they ever do any work there?' I asked.

'No, they just go to see what they can find or beg. Sometimes they take something to sell. Quite a lot of Kaiwa have got lazy about planting. They've become scroungers,'. . . and I added mentally, 'And they've also lost their dignity.'

It was clear from the way these Indians spoke that they deplored the situation as much as we did. We also wondered what effects this kind of thing was going to have on the children of such families, left to their own devices day after day. Perhaps we will only know when it is too late.

Amazingly enough the little girl's burns healed almost without a scar. The only thing to do in cases like this is to go to their houses. Sometimes when I needed to visit a sick person I would go on foot with one of my children for company, not only because this was culturally necessary, but because it was helpful to have someone to hold things. This kind of ministry always made the bond with the family in question stronger, but it was hard not to be critical of the way of life that led to many of the wounds and sicknesses we treated.

Those days, I remember, were hectic—filled with activity

from morning to night. In between the translation, medical and educational work, one had to find time just to be unhurried with people, as well as coping with the mechanics of living in a more or less primitive situation. Cooking, washing and cleaning all took longer than they do in city life, and there were days when I was so tired that, if I shut my eyes to pray with the children at night, I would fall asleep.

Small wonder that during the week I have just described, I never had time to sweep the house. Dust began to collect accusingly around the corners of our bedroom. I kept thinking: 'I must sweep this room. I can't let it go until our big Saturday cleaning session.' Particularly annoying was a small piece of blue cloth which had fallen on the floor beside the bed. I thought it was a strip left over from our sewing class (I was making patchwork quilts with the women). As the week wore on it gathered more and more dust, and I remember saying to myself; 'I must get rid of that silly little piece of blue cloth. Why don't I just sweep it out of the house, or pick it up and put it in the fire?' But always there was something more pressing.

A moment came when I couldn't stand it any longer. I grabbed the broom and started to sweep the red concrete floor. I was just about to sweep the little piece of blue cloth out of the door, along with all the dust and dirt, when something made me bend down and pick it up. I shook off the dust and examined it. It wasn't just any old piece of blue cloth as I had thought; it was a carefully cut strip, shaped to a point at one end, and I realized then that it was a bookmark that one of my children had made and given to me. It had dropped from my Bible. As I smoothed it out, I read the words that my child had carefully written in black ink on it:

Love never gives up (1 Corinthians 13:7 GNB).

It was God's Word to me. It came so directly, so clearly, that He might have been looking over my shoulder, reading it.

And then I saw that in spite of all the heartache of working at Armadillo Water, there was no opting out—because 'Love *never* gives up.' I knew without any doubt that we had to stay where we were.

11

What happened to the scissors?

Gloria lived close to Hortensia's family. She was another of those who suffered as the winds of change blew over Armadillo Water. I sometimes wondered how she could have been so inappropriately named, and even as I write this, I am inspired to pray that the end of her life may yet be glorious, because her early life has, without doubt, been singularly lacking in glory.

She was widowed during our absence from the tribe, when her husband was killed in a drunken brawl. It did not make matters any easier when it was discovered that his killer was the sixteen-year-old cousin of Hortensia, who was, as it were, Gloria's next-door-neighbour. The boy had been so drunk that he had no recollection of the event, which had taken place outside one of the small wayside stores that sold *pinga* illegally to Indians.

After I heard the story, I took out our book of Kaiwa snapshots, and turned to a picture of Michael sitting beside this same boy. They used to play together. Staring at it, I was overwhelmed with sadness.

Without a husband a Kaiwa woman has quite a struggle, especially if she has a large family. Gloria had a staircase of children, from a twenty-year-old daughter to a babe-in-sling. Her daughter also had two children and was now totally dependent on Gloria, since her own irresponsible husband had walked out on her some months previously.

I had been told by the wife of a Brazilian farmer that Gloria was trying hard to keep her family together by washing clothes for people or helping with odd jobs. I understood that she was a good worker. So when she came to ask me if she could do some work, I arranged for her to come during the week to do some cleaning and washing. I had been given a sack of good used clothes, so I decided to pass these on to Gloria along with the money I would pay her.

She arrived promptly on the appointed day and set to work with a will. I should explain that this arrangement is quite different from having an English charwoman. For one thing she brings her baby, which she feeds whenever it cries. When she is not feeding it, there must be someone to hold the baby, so an older child comes as the 'baby-sitter'. On this occasion Gloria also brought her daughter to help with the washing, who in turn brought her two children. They, too, had to have baby-sitters. Usually the baby-sitters follow the 'workers' around wherever they go, thus tracking an unnecessary amount of dirt through the house; but never mind, that is how they operate. Then they all have to be fed. All things considered, I probably could have done the work more quickly myself—but that would not have helped Gloria.

At the end of the day, when I gave her the clothes and her payment, she was delighted. She took a quick look at the garments and soon had it all worked out as to what would do for whom.

She went off in high spirits.

* * *

The next afternoon I expected my women's class. They came a little after noon and we spent the first hour reading, and learning new letters. Then we turned to writing. After practising the new letters and some simple sentences, I gave them a short dictation. As they concentrated hard on these new skills I would look around the group amazed that some of them could produce such good work with one hand, while their other hand was busy controlling a baby. Occasionally the baby-sitters would manage to get two of the babies to sleep in the hammock—top to tail.

After the literacy class we turned to sewing. They were making patchwork covers for their babies, and we all thoroughly enjoyed chatting as we sewed. At one point when we needed to cut out more hexagons, I went inside to find the scissors. They were not in any of the usual places.

'What happened to the scissors?' The question was

addressed to the rest of my family, but no one knew. It happened that, apart from a pair of surgical scissors which were kept separate for obvious reasons, they were the only scissors I had. I hunted high and low for them and finally began to think back to the last time I had used them.

Then I remembered. I had distinctly seen them the previous day on the back verandah. I had been putting patches on the children's jeans. I remembered that it was on this same table that Gloria had put the sack of clothes while she gathered her family together before leaving.

'Could it be that she took my scissors?' As the day wore on I became convinced that this is what had happened.

I felt somehow betrayed and I said to the Lord: 'Here I am trying to help Gloria and how does she repay me?—by walking off with my scissors. I really can't get along without my scissors, especially for the sewing class. I've got to get those scissors back.' I was quite steamed up. I thought of all sorts of schemes such as you might find in detective stories to discover if Gloria really had taken the scissors, and then there was the problem of getting them back. Having been with the Kaiwa as long as we had, we knew it was fatal to accuse them, even if you were certain. The truth was I did not know how to handle this situation and still have Gloria as a friend. On the other hand, if I ignored it, our friendship would continue on a rather rocky basis.

'If any of you lacks wisdom, let him ask God . . . and it will be given him' (James 1:5 RSV). I knew I needed help, but there were a few things to straighten out first . . . .

When I really let Him in, He went right to the heart of the matter—'Whose are the scissors anyway?' After a moment's reflection I had to answer: 'They're Yours, Lord. Everything I possess is Yours.'

Then He showed me what to do.

A few days later, some of Gloria's family came to visit us. They sat on the front verandah doing puzzles, looking at magazines, talking . . . I looked round the group. One of the girls had been with Gloria when she had come to work for me, so I waited for an opportune moment to ask her:

'Did your mother borrow the scissors the other day when she was here? The ones I left on the table at the back? Because as it happens, I don't have any more scissors and I need to use them.'

'Yes, she did,' the girl said. 'She needed them to alter some of the clothes you gave her so that they would fit the little ones.'

'That's fine,' I said. 'If she could send them back to me soon, I would be grateful. And any time she wants to use them again, tell her just to let me know.'

She brought back the scissors the very next day, and our relationship was not jeopardized. But even more precious to me was the fact that I had lacked wisom, I had asked for it, and God had given it to me.

12

Three palm trees

The strident note of the bell-bird rang out from the patch of jungle opposite our front verandah. We jumped up to see if we could catch a glimpse of it. Against the background of a brilliant blue sky we saw it, perching on a branch of the tallest tree, the sun lighting up its pure white plumage and its naked blue throat. It seemed incongruous that such a beautiful bird should have such a harsh call. Named by some Brazilians as the 'Blacksmith bird', its note sounds for all the world like the ring of steel on steel—the blacksmith's hammer striking the anvil.

That particular patch of jungle was the backcloth for many exotic tropical birds: toucans with long, brilliantly painted bills; the soft olives, blues and burnished gold of tanagers; the yellow-breasted *bem-te-vi*—'glad-to-have-seen-you' bird, with its smart hat of black-and-white stripes; the sudden red flash of the rarely seen macaws; and the vivid green parrots that flew over in twos and threes just before sunset.

Nearer at hand we had the humming-birds. There was the brown 'hermit' with a tapered, white-fringed tail, who became so at home with us that he built his nest on a slender piece of grass hanging down from our roof. Have you ever thought what an amazing feat of engineering that is—to build a nest so that it hangs evenly, when it is only attached on one side? This ingenious little bird, using spider's silk, fastens weights of mud or pebbles under the nest directly beneath the point of attachment in order to redress the balance. Our hermit would fly in through the open window and hover over the breakfast table, and the Indians told us that we were favoured because the gods pay their visits in the form of humming-birds.

Armadillo Water was still a very beautiful place, and I was always grateful that some of the jungle near to us had been

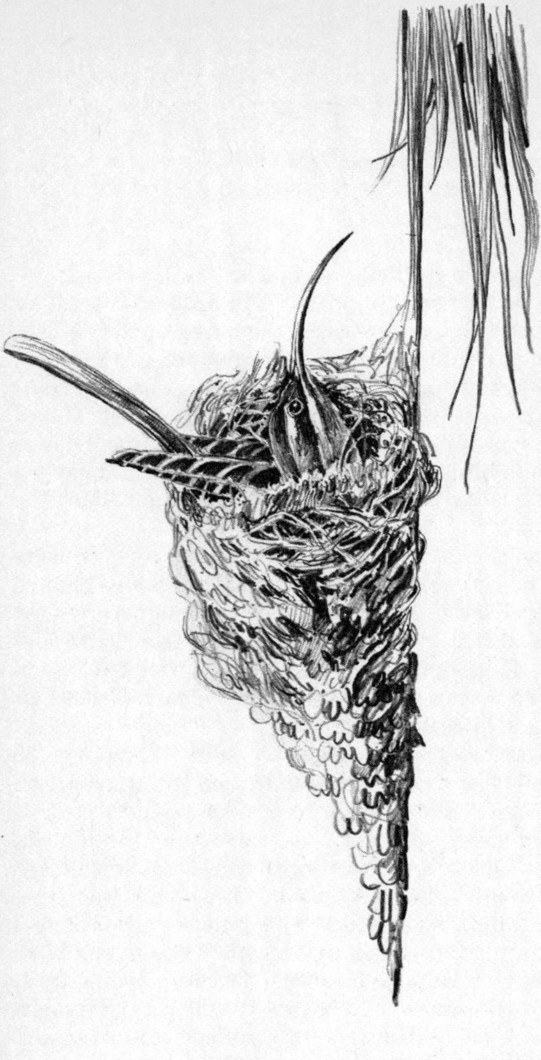

Hermit humming-bird in its nest
which is suspended by one piece of grass.

preserved in its pristine glory so that we could enjoy it.

The other three sides of the house overlooked the fields of neighbouring Brazilian farms. The views were not so inspiring and changed from season to season, depending on what crops had been planted. But in the midst of all this change there was one thing that did not change. It was a group of three palm trees growing together, tall and graceful, their fronds faithfully reflecting the moods of the weather. I could see them from my kitchen window, and whenever crops were cut or land cleared or fields burned in readiness for planting, I always silently pleaded with the farmers not to cut down those three palm trees. They never did, at least not while I was there, and I was very glad, because for me they stood for something special.

*   *   *

While we rejoiced over the glories of God's creation, we also rejoiced over His re-creations. Avelino was one of them. When he was converted through the witness of another Indian, he changed almost over night. From being a drunken layabout, he became a hard-working fearless Christian. He built a shelter at the side of his house where his neighbours could come and hear the Gospel preached. It was quite usual for fifty to sixty Indians to gather in his little 'church' on Sundays.

When a Brazilian friend of ours heard that he had been converted, she could not believe it. Before she moved away from the area, she had seen him more often drunk than sober. She asked about him several times to make sure he was the same man. The change in him could only be attributed to the transforming work of God's Spirit.

His wife, Miriam, was a believer too. She supported him in all his Christian activities, and as we were often invited by them to help with services, I got to know her quite well.

One day, as we were talking together, she suddenly said: 'Do you remember how sick Alicia was?' With her chin she indicated her youngest daughter, who was playing with her little brother a few yards from the house.

'No,' I said, 'I don't remember. Tell me about it.'

She looked at me incredulously and said: 'Surely you remember. She was just a baby at the time and she was very ill.

We thought she was going to die. We didn't know Jesus in those days. Someone told us that you would give us medicine for her, so I took her to your house. There were lots of people there that day, don't you remember?'

It was beginning to come back to me. There had been a time about five years before, when there was an epidemic of measles. Babies were particularly vulnerable. On top of this there had been a lot of diarrhoea, vomiting, and also eye infections, particularly among babies. I had treated so many that I had no clear recollection any more of individual cases.

'Yes, Miriam,' I said, 'I think I can remember the time, but there were so many sick babies then, that I can't quite remember Alicia.'

'Well,' she said, 'I didn't know you before that day. I'd only heard about you. I told you how sick my baby was and asked you for medicine. I explained how she hadn't been able to sleep for nights and the whole family was exhausted because of it.'

'Now I remember!' I said, and there flashed into my mind the picture of a distraught mother and her child. I had talked to her under the trees that day, because the house had been so full of people. I had taken the medicine out there to the baby.

It had been a frightening time in a way, because one of Basilio's relatives, ironically called 'John the Baptist', had set himself up as a witchdoctor almost opposite our house. He held nightly healing sessions, with chanting and rattle-shaking. So many babies had died under his care that a kind of panic had swept the village. We felt we were walking on a knife edge.

As Miriam and I talked together about all that had happened, she said to me: 'The medicine you gave Alicia was good, but it isn't so much the medicine that I remember, but the prayer you prayed that day. You asked Jesus to make her well and cause her to sleep. That night she slept all night for the first time in weeks.'

Avelino loved to sing. Whenever we visited him, no matter what the day or hour, he would never let us go without singing two or three hymns and praying.

One day when we went to see him he said: 'Sit down, John. Sit down, younger-aunt. I want to tell you about the dream I

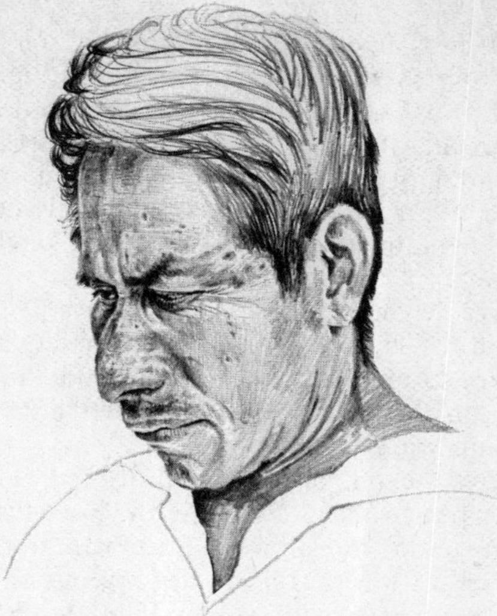

Avelino.

had last night:

'There were a lot of Kaiwa gathered in a big open place, and we were all singing hymns. Suddenly, as we were singing, we saw that Jesus was standing in the middle of us. When the hymn was finished, Jesus took a book and handed it to me. It was Mark's Gospel in Kaiwa. He said to me: "Take this book, Avelino, and study it. If you live by this book, you will live well. You will live in a way that pleases me, and I will bless you and your family."

'Then,' said Avelino, 'We all started to sing again. This time we sang, "Take the name of Jesus with you," [which is, incidentally, Avelino's favourite hymn]. And I looked, and saw that Jesus was singing it too . . . in *my* language. Wasn't that wonderful? Then He slowly went up into the sky, and as He disappeared, all of us who were left turned to each other with joy on our faces and embraced each other.'

Avelino was obviously very moved by this dream.

On days like this it wasn't very hard for me to praise the Lord, to lift my heart to Him—it came quite naturally. And on the desperately hard days I was united to Him by the bond of my helplessness, my need. But on some of the very ordinary days, the busy days, when I went from one thing to the other without time to breathe, then I found it all too easy to forget Him. Especially if, added to the ordinary things, there were the extraordinary irritations: the fire smoked; or the clothes-line broke; or an Indian caller systematically demolished all her neighbours' reputations; then my gaze rarely rose above ground level.

Whatever the day had been like I always had to end up in the kitchen to prepare supper. Just at the hour when day is giving place to night, several things would happen. For one thing, the tiny biting flies would descend, attacking legs and arms. In time you get used to that.

As I stirred the soup or prepared the rice, the kitchen shutter would be open so that I could use the last of the daylight. I would stare out of it towards the three palm trees—and then I would catch my breath. Like some gorgeous oil painting, the sky would be alive with colour, and the palm trees, so strikingly silhouetted against it, became the focal point of this glory. Their blackness made the gold more gold and the red more red. The flames of the sunset would seem like long arms stretched out towards me invitingly, and the Creator of it all would say: 'Come back to me, daughter, and let us enjoy a few moments together.'

And every one of these moments was unique, because the sunset constantly changed, as is its wont—and the three palm trees, silhouetted against it, stood witness to it all. Here was something that baffled my human mind. However much I had neglected Him all day, He would still put on this lavish display of beauty and offer it to me as a love-gift. It moved me as nothing else could.

* * *

This cameo is quite exquisite. It is, perhaps, the most special of all to me. Through it I am reminded that God's love for me is both constant and extravagant. It does not ebb and flow to the rhythm of my fickleness, nor does it ever count the cost. It is so much more effective in showing me my failures and inspiring my devotion to Christ than any rebuke or exhortation

The three palm trees,
as seen from Audrey's kitchen.

could ever be. And it has become a standard towards which I must strive in showing love to others.

It speaks to me, Lord,
This sunset of Yours—
You painted it with living strokes of fire
On the wide canvas of the sky,
Telling me that You love beauty,
You love variety,
You love movement and life.
You show the infinite wealth
Of Your creativity
Just to me
In this moment of time,
For my enjoyment,
For my encouragement—
To call my spirit to Yours
In worship.

(1973)

13

I brought you my baby . . .

It was Sunday afternoon, and as usual we cleared away after lunch, shut our eyes for a few minutes, and prepared to set out for Elidio's house. We knew that they would have swept the floor, dusted the benches and gathered the neighbours together, in readiness for the weekly meeting. These meetings had become a regular part of their lives, and we were always sure of an attentive audience as we told stories of Jesus, illustrated with flannelgraph pictures. Only in this way could we effectively hold the attention of toddlers and grandmothers as well, and we knew there would be both of these age groups present, as well as all the ages in between.

I remember that afternoon so clearly. We had actually got out of the door, flannelgraph material under our arms, when we saw the little family group coming, single file, up the track to our house. As far as we could tell, we had never seen them before.

My heart sank. I never quite knew where my priorities lay when this kind of thing happened. So often folk dropped in to look at magazines or because they wanted us to take their photograph—nothing urgent. But on this occasion I was left in no doubt.

The little group arrived, breathless, and the baby in the mother's arms was completely covered with a cloth. She didn't waste any time over complaints about the weather, but burst out immediately: 'I brought you my baby . . . Can you do something to save my child?'

She removed the cloth and showed me an eight-month-old baby girl, burning with fever, her breath coming in gasps. The eyes were half closed and only the whites were showing.

'How long has she been sick?'

'Seven days.'

It was useless to say: 'Why didn't you bring her sooner?' because it wouldn't have helped the present situation, and in any case we knew the answer: they had tried the witchdoctor and probably a hotch-potch of jungle remedies (some of which can be quite effective); they did not want to take her to the Mission hospital; finally they had heard about us.

So John and the children took the bundle of flannelgraph materials and went off to the meeting, and I said: 'Let's go inside.'

We were fortunate in having a friend staying with us at this time, Jill Oakey, a former Wycliffe member and a nurse. Jill stayed behind with me, and we did our best for the baby. After bathing her to bring down the fever and giving her medicine, we prayed together. I told the young mother about Jesus, about how He healed the sick when He was on earth. I explained how He was alive today and still had that same power. In her desperate concern for her baby she repeated after me every word of the prayer I offered.

The baby's breathing became easier and her eyes opened and she looked at us. The young mother was ecstatic. We put the baby in our hammock for a while and she slept peacefully.

During this time we learned something about the family. I made some sweet herb tea, the way they like it, and gradually some of the tensions of the last few days slipped away. She told us of where she lived, indicating the direction with her chin. With such a vague description I did not feel very confident about finding her house if ever I should want to. She also explained that her husband was away working on a Brazilian farm, and that he would not return until the end of the month. For this reason her father had accompanied her.

After a while she stood up and said: 'I'm about to be going again.' I tried to persuade her to stay, so that we could keep an eye on the baby— if necessary she could stay all night. But she was quite sure that the baby would be all right—'Look, she is sleeping peacefully. She is not burning with fever any more. Her breathing is easy.' In a flush of optimism, she took the baby out of the hammock and put her, still sleeping, in the sling over her shoulder, gathered together the rest of the family and bid us goodbye.

On an impulse I said: 'Let us come with you, so we'll know

where your house is.'

'Good,' she said, 'Come. We'd like to show you our house. Then you'll be able to visit us again another day.'

So we followed the little procession as it moved swiftly down the track, and then turned off through the jungle, along narrow trails, sometimes to the left, sometimes to the right, until finally we arrived at their home.

The extended family was quite large, and it surged forward *en masse* to see how the baby was. We sat with them and talked for a while, and then as I looked at the sun which was fast approaching the horizon, I said: 'The afternoon is already old. We are about to be going again.'

Back home Jill and I were still very concerned about the baby, and this concern grew as the evening wore on. So we took a flashlight and more medicine and set off to find the house.

The night was black and starless. As we passed the silent shapes of sleeping Indian houses, dogs yapped and roosters crowed prematurely. A harsh whisper within usually restored the peace. It was embarrassing to be disturbing so many families.

I laughed at my stupidity in memorizing the path by my usual method: 'Take the right fork at the twisted tree, and the left fork at the group of banana palms. . . .' By divine guidance rather than by my skill, we eventually arrived.

The baby was in the centre of a dimly lit circle of agitated relatives all proffering advice. As we approached someone was trying vainly to spoon a milky mixture from a dirty old tin can into the unyielding lips of the baby. The grandfather was blowing through cupped hands on to her head. 'How is she?' I asked unnecessarily. It was obvious that she was much worse. Every few minutes, someone who thought they knew what to do would snatch the baby and take over the proceedings.

'If we don't get this baby away from here,' Jill whispered to me, 'she won't last the night out. Can't we get her to the hospital?' I hesitated. I did not want to put pressure on them to take her against their will, so I prayed silently for a moment or two. 'Are you sure you wouldn't like to take her to the Mission hospital?' I asked. 'There they have many more medicines and facilities for taking care of sick people. What do you think?'

There followed a hubbub of rapid conversation. Everyone was talking at the same time. The pros and cons were being thoroughly discussed and I lost track of the argument. Then suddenly the young mother turned to me and said:

'Yes, we'll go. We really have confidence in you. If you say it is good to go, then we'll go.'

She pulled a sack from somewhere up in the rafters and began to rummage in it. Then she took out a pair of crumpled trousers and a jacket and handed them over to her father. He put them on over his other clothes. She also pulled out an equally crumpled cotton blouse and skirt and put them on over her own clothes. After fixing the baby securely in the sling again, we were ready to go. We went back to our house to get the Land Rover.

John felt it best to stay with our children so that Jill and I could see the matter through. As we bumped along the dirt road, the baby's grandfather continued his ministration from the back of the car. He would lean over from time to time and blow hard through his hand on to the crown of the baby's head, and then continue muttering what I suppose were some kind of prayers. Jill kept her finger on the baby's pulse. At one point I felt her stiffen and then after a tense moment, relax.

'The heart stopped beating,' she whispered, 'but it's all right now. It's started again.'

I kept my eyes on the road, trying to avoid the worst pot-holes without losing speed. I was so thankful that we now had a Land Rover, and my mind went back to Elidio's slow journey in the *charrete* all those years before.

'Lord, glorify Your name again,' I prayed, 'as You did when Elidio's life hung in the balance.'

We arrived at the hospital and explained the situation to the nurse on duty. Diagnosing bronchial pneumonia, she realized that there was no time to lose. She gave the baby medication by means of an injection and a suppository, which the young mother did not understand at all. I explained in Kaiwa how suppositories worked, and thereafter found myself explaining everything that happened to her. The nurses only spoke Portuguese.

They quickly fixed up a steam tent to help to alleviate the baby's breathing difficulties. But the grandfather would break into the steam tent every few minutes to blow on the baby's head. The nurses were very patient and tried to explain to him that he must leave the baby alone, but after several unsuccessful attempts, I offered to take him home, leaving only the mother there with her baby.

When we got back, he got out of the Land Rover where his track went off to the left. As I looked at the black jungle ahead of him, I offered to lend him my flashlight. He took it gratefully, and I knew he would return it in due course.

As it happened he came back with it the next morning. I was on our crowded front verandah dispensing medicine, when I saw him coming up the path.

I didn't need to ask him what had happened. His very gait told me; and when I put out my hand to greet him, he put both arms around me and then 'lifted up his voice and wept'. As his tears splashed on to my shoulder, mine fell on to that same black jacket that I had seen him put on the night before. Between the sobs he told me what had happened. The heartbroken young mother was already back at home with her still, white bundle; and some of the extended family were saying: 'I told you so!' Without much difficulty they had all totally misunderstood every effort that the nurses, and later the doctor, had made to save the baby's life.

Finally he took the flashlight from his pocket and handed it to me. As he took his leave, it was clear that he bore me no ill will. He turned and set off slowly back to his mourning family, and I watched him until he disappeared, ignoring the questions the other Indians were asking, because there were so many questions hammering in my own head, demanding an answer.

I had no heart for any more medical work that day. Jill stepped into the breach and John acted as interpreter, and they kindly handled everything for me.

As I mechanically cooked the food and bathed the children, I asked myself a thousand questions, and wished a thousand times that I had done things differently. Above all things I wished I had not taken the baby to the Mission hospital. There was now one more example that could be used as fuel for those who were bent on destroying the hospital's reputation.

But behind all these question was the one that I didn't want to ask: 'Lord, why did You let it happen? Why didn't You use the opportunity like you did in Elidio's case, to demonstrate Your power to these people?

'Why did You let the Mission hospital, with its already shaky reputation, be further discredited? I would have done anything to have saved these colleagues this further disgrace. They, who had given themselves for the Indians, and had always helped and encouraged us whenever we needed them . . . surely, Lord, they deserve better than this. It doesn't make sense to me, Lord. It would have been so wonderful if the baby had recovered.'

Lying on my bed that night and staring into the darkness because sleep wouldn't come, I told Him just what I felt, summing it up with: '. . . I simply don't understand You, Lord.'

* * *

'Dear child, I don't ask you to understand Me (how could you?), only to *trust* Me. If you believe you are acting in obedience to My will, then I take responsibility for the consequences. Remember that My ways are not your ways, neither are My thoughts your thoughts. I am trustworthy, child, so learn to trust Me, even when you don't understand.'

And just as I could see nothing as I gazed up into the darkness, but knew that the house was there, strong and secure, sheltering me from the night wind and the weather, so I realized that it was a necessary ingredient of faith to trust in the dark—to trust when I couldn't see. To trust Him, when I didn't understand His ways, was the highest vote of confidence I could give Him.

So a gleam of light seemed to shine in the blackness; a new star of understanding was born.

And if He was in all things to be trusted, this did not mean only where I was concerned. I could trust Him for others too. It meant He was present in the young mother's darkness and had purposes of love for her, even in the middle of the ache. I had to trust her to Him also.

As I finally closed my eyes, I lifted her and all her bewildered family to Him and craved for them a special blessing. Then, comforted, I fell asleep.

14

Shadows after Dawn

Some lessons are slowly learned. No doubt that is why Jesus gave me cameos with an enduring quality about them. I often needed to take them out and look at them, remembering the lessons they taught me. This was especially true of the one I described in the last chapter, and I found that this and also the banana-palm principle needed a considerable amount of underlining. I needed them both in connection with a certain Kaiwa woman. . . .

* * *

"I'll be the one!" Aurora said, with a smile that reached from one ear to the other. She reminded me so much of her mother when she smiled.

I had reached the stage where teaching two of my own children, looking after the third and continuing with language work and literacy—not to mention the inglorious but necessary business of housekeeping—were becoming a bit too much for me. John and I had talked about the possibility of having a Kaiwa girl come and help me for a few hours every day, thinking that we would also get the added advantage of more language practice through this arrangement.

Somehow the subject came up one day when Aurora was visiting us. I believe she asked us a leading question. The result was that she came with her mother the following day to talk it over. Just in case it all worked out she brought all her worldly possessions with her . . . wrapped in a headscarf. We finally made an arrangement that did not uproot her from her home and family. She spent the morning hours with us and left after lunch.

Aurora was fifteen at the time. Her mother, Turira, was a

radiant woman who had quite a story to tell. Apparently all her early pregnancies had ended in still-born babies. But while she was carrying Aurora, she had come in contact with the Kaiwa Mission and had got to know Loide Andrade. Turira spoke so little Portuguese that she was hardly able to understand the services at the Mission church, but Loide had learned sufficient Kaiwa through her long years of experience with this tribe to enable her to talk with Turira in her own language. She assured her that she would ask Jesus to cause this next baby to live. Her prayer was answered and Aurora ('Dawn') was born. She was so named because her birth signified the dawn of a new era in Turira's life. After that she bore many children. In fact she became a by-word among the other women. So much so that years later, when I was speaking about the second coming of Christ in the Kaiwa women's class one Sunday morning, there was consternation followed by howls of laughter at the thought of Turira, pregnant as usual, going up to meet the Lord. 'How would she ever get off the ground?' they said. Turira laughed as heartily as everbody else.

But Turira's experience of Jesus did not end there. Life was hard for her and her husband, Osirio, as their family grew. And then one day tragedy struck, and Osirio became so sick that Turira knew he would soon die. She thought of all the problems that face a Kaiwa woman without a husband—problems which I have learned to appreciate only very gradually —and in desperation she knelt on the hard-packed earth floor of her simple home, clasped her hands together and looked up to the roof:

'Jesus, if You are really there and if You can hear me, I plead with you to heal my husband. You know what will become of me if he dies. Cause him to live again.'

And He did. Osirio took a turn for the better from that hour and Turira became radiantly certain that Jesus was real, that He could hear when you called Him, and that He had power over sickness. She asked Him to be her Saviour.

She was very happy when Aurora came to work for us. To her it seemed like another answer to prayer. For us it was a new experience, not without its anxious moments. On the first morning I gave her simple jobs to do, such as sweeping, wash-

Turira with a young child.

ing up and preparing vegetables. As our wood-burning stove had collapsed we were using a calor-gas stove that had been lent to us, and so I told Aurora that I would do the cooking, knowing that she would be unfamiliar with a gas stove. I put four pans on the four burners to cook our midday meal of beans, rice, squash and stew, and then went back to my two small boys who were doing sums. Aurora was busy sweeping outside the house.

At about noon she came to get me. 'It's all soft [cooked],' she said. 'Are you going to eat now?' I followed her as she turned back to the kitchen. There was a rather nauseating smell of gas. As I checked the stove, I discovered all four gas knobs were turned on, but not one of them was alight. Having ascertained that the food was cooked, she had simply blown them all out. Before the next lunch-time I taught her how to use the stove!

When someone heard that Aurora was coming to help me, they made a rather graphic scooping gesture with their hand, ending up with it behind their back. It was used to indicate that someone was a thief, so I took the precaution of saying on the first day: 'Look, Aurora, I don't expect you to take anything home that doesn't belong to you. But if you want something just ask me and I'll do my best to help you.'

I suppose in some ways we watched her like a hawk, poor thing, but in all the six months she worked for us, she never betrayed my trust in her. Sometimes she would ask to take the left-over food home to her family, and sometimes she would ask for new sandals, for sweet-smelling toilet soap, or for needle and thread. We were more than pleased to give her these things.

After she had said goodbye on her last day (we were leaving to attend a conference), I missed a teaspoon. It may seem a small thing but all the same I was disappointed. I hoped and hoped that my suspicions would not be confirmed. Looking back on it now I am ashamed that I doubted her. The teaspoon turned up in the grass outside the house where the washing-up water had been thrown out of the plastic bowl.

Time went on and Aurora got married and moved away, but my friendship with Turira deepened. She was such a blessing to me. She showed concern for me in so many ways and for my family too. One day when she came to help me translate some hymns, she asked how my children were. I told her that my daughter, Anne, had a fever and was not at all well. Before she left for home that day she went in to see Anne, and standing beside her bed she prayed for her. She grew to love Anne and later taught her how to weave.

On another occasion she came, knowing I was expecting her, even though she had not slept all night because of severe toothache. I hardly recognized her as she arrived saying: 'How is your afternoon?' Her face was hugely swollen at one side, and her eyes told the story of pain, but she was still smiling. Instead of working with her I made some soft macaroni and then took her to the hospital. Her uncomplaining attitude was an inspiration to me.

I learned a lot of interesting titbits from Turira as we chatted day after day. One of these incidents underlined to me once again the need for Scripture in a people's mother tongue—a consistent yardstick in written form by means of which beliefs can be measured. This is perhaps the most important way to guard against syncretism, the mixing of the Christian faith with tribal beliefs.

Turira was telling me about the death of Rosinha, one of our very first language helpers. She had died while we were out of the tribe, and the fact was communicated to me without ceremony on the first Sunday we were back with the Indians. As I came to her name in the register of the Kaiwa women's class, I noticed with a stab of sadness that there was a line through it, and the word *morreu* (she died) after it.

Rosinha had been very sick. She had been in the Mission hospital, but her relatives had taken her out ('That's why she died,' said Turira), and she herself had been hopeful of recovery. When Turira went to visit her the second time, even before she arrived at the house, she heard wailing, and then met Rosinha's daughter and other members of the family, wandering up and down the path. When it was time for the burial, they put all her personal belongings into the shallow grave with her, believing she would need them in the next life. Turira enumerated the things they buried—her clothes, her bowl and spoon, her cross and rattles, her pipe, her hammock . . . and her 'Biblia' wrapped up in a cloth and placed inside the blouse she was wearing. Her granddaughter said: 'We don't know this paper, but our Mother knows it and she will want to have it with her where she is going.' Then she chided her brothers and uncles for getting drunk on the occasion of their mother's funeral. She told them that it would be much better if they followed the ways of *Nhandejary* (God our Chief) rather than getting drunk.

As Turira returned from the funeral with her own family she said: 'Listen, children, you can't take anything with you when you die: just your spirit (your past words) goes to God. It's no good burying anything with a person.'

'And then,' Turira added to me, 'I waited at home listening for the thunder. I knew that when Rosinha arrived at God's place she would let me know through the thunder. I waited and waited, and then at the end of the second afternoon, just as the sun was setting, I heard it—the rumble of thunder in the west, and I was happy because I knew she had arrived.'

* * *

'Turira,' I said one day, 'sometimes you tell me about the plants you and your people use to make medicine. I'd really like to learn more about them. Will you teach me? I'd like to make a book about these wise things.'

'I'd be happy to teach you,' she said. 'Many of the young people don't know these things any more. If you wrote about them in a book, then they wouldn't be forgotten.

'A little while before my mother died, when she was old and her hair was white like cotton, she took me into the jungle and taught me all she knew about the healing plants. I will teach you all she taught me.'

That was how we began a very fascinating study. Turira shared her knowledge with me, bringing samples of each plant she described, unfolding to me the wisdom of this jungle people. As I checked what I learned with other Kaiwa I found a surprising degree of consistency, and it seemed that most of the remedies were effective. There were in fact one or two more fanciful remedies, for example the one especially used by youths. If they bathed their arms in the water made from boiling the leaves of a certain tree, it was claimed they would always score a direct hit with bow and arrow. But on the whole medicines were used for common illnesses.

One day I asked her: 'Turira, why do your people ask all the time for white man's medicine nowadays? Why don't they still use the plant medicines?'

In reply she told me: 'Some people still use our old remedies, but we know they have their limitations. There are some diseases like TB that we don't know how to cure. We need white man's medicine for those sicknesses. Sometimes our remedies help but don't cure—like the time I was bitten by a snake. My mother wrapped a banana leaf round the bite, because the sap is an effective antidote, but she still took me to the hospital. All the way as we were going there she kept asking me: "Can you taste the poison in your mouth yet? Can you smell it in your nose?" And I would say: "No, Mother." Then she would say: "Good, then there's hope. But once you've tasted the poison in your mouth then there is no hope." Because she took me to the hospital in time, I got better.'

Then she added: 'But many people don't use the healing plants because they don't know them well enough, and it is a lot of work to find them and prepare them. Sometimes we have to get help quickly and haven't time to go into the jungle looking for plants and trees. That's why more and more people are using white man's medicine.

'And then there's another thing,' said Turira, and certainly to her this was significant. 'Sometimes these things are used in connection with rattle-shaking and calling on the spirits. We who are believers don't want to do that anymore. When I give people our herbal medicine I always pray for them. I tell them that it is God who heals and that often He uses the plants He has caused to grow, to effect a cure.'

* * *

During the weeks we studied herb-lore together, the shadows were gathering over Turira's home. Her husband, Osirio, no longer accompanied her to the Kaiwa Mission services. He had become bitter against the Mission, claiming that they did not help him materially. This was not true, but certainly Osirio had the idea that he should receive many more benefits from his association with the Mission than in fact came his way. He began to transfer his attention from the Mission to the local *bolicho*. He came home drunk more and more often.

Turira was very loyal to him and rarely said anything about these lapses, but one day it was all too much for her, and she told me everything. She told me how she often had to go with her children into the jungle behind her house to escape Osirio's violence, and that one day she had returned home to find that he had burned all her clothes. She asked that we should pray about it.

But the shadows were to become deeper, and what happened next occurred during one of the times we were not in the tribe. Turira told me about it afterwards and I heard substantially the same story from other people. She became the victim of circumstances completely beyond her control. When Osirio went to the Indian police to say that he no longer wanted her as his wife, she knew she was faced with several frightening consequences. One was that she effectively lost all her children. I had already seen this aspect of Kaiwa culture at work on other occasions. Usually if a Kaiwa widow remarries, she cannot take her children with her. She must find someone else, such as her parents if they are living, to take care of them. If, however, her new husband is a widower with his own children, she is required to look after them for him, but without the usual maternal right. Turira became to all intents and purposes a widow.

She also knew that the Indian police, knowing that she was without a husband, would deem it their duty to find her a suitable one, probably a widower or a man abandoned by his wife, who had children of his own and who needed someone to cook the food and wash the clothes.

As a Christian Turira did not wish to be given to another man. She stayed for a while with a Christian Kaiwa family who were sympathetic to her situation. The 'authorities' did not however let the matter rest there. It was considered irregular and, moreover, they had a widower with two children already lined up for her. They put a great deal of pressure on her until she finally gave in.

We heard that Turira had married again almost as soon as we arrived back on the scene. I was a little bit puzzled and certainly did not know all that lay behind that deceivingly simple statement, which incidentally came to us in Portuguese. When she knew we were back she came to see me and so I asked her:

'Turira, have you married again?' When she said no, I was even more puzzled. On top of everything else, was she lying to me? Looking back I am again ashamed. My knowledge of the language, although quite considerable by this time, did not stretch to the vagaries of Kaiwa marriage relationships. Only by accident did I later discover that certainly Turira had not 'married again' – that would have meant that she had gone back and remarried Osirio. So that was why she had patiently explained to me again that Osirio wasn't interested in having her as his wife any more. What she had actually done was 'married newly'. She had married a husband new to her. I had not asked her the right question.

Turira was doing her best to be a good wife and 'mother' in this new household. She described her new husband as hard-working and kind to her. The two children were no trouble to her. But she was worried about her own children—I could see the pain in her eyes—and I had heard that they were lacking her maternal care. Osirio had a new wife, too, apparently, a young thing who liked doing the things he liked to do. She was not very interested in the children. In all aspects of this drama, Kaiwa culture was strongly against Turira.

As I thought about all that had happened, I was not surprised that Turira was no longer attending the Mission church where she had come to know the Lord and where she had received so much teaching and care. When she talked about it she said it was a long way away from where she now lived, but I knew there were deeper reasons. Who but the Lord Himself can sort out all the cross-cultural misunderstandings that arise between members of Christ's body, especially when they don't speak the same language? There are too many imponderables. It's like trying to make an intersection between roads that run along different levels. As things stood I could see that she couldn't go back. She didn't know how to straighten out the tangle.

The one gleam of light in the blackness was that she knew so many hymns and choruses by heart. She had learned them through her long years of association with the Mission and through her work on hymn translation with me. But sadly she was cut off from the comfort of those portions of the Word of God that existed in her own language because she couldn't read. She was only in the very early stages of literacy when all this took place.

* * *

I do not know fully why Turira left her second husband. She said that he got tired of her. They moved to another Kaiwa reservation for a while and eventually she came back to live a somewhat rootless life by herself. I have never seen her since this happened. Various disquieting rumours reached us and we didn't know which to believe, but whatever was true, I found my heart going out in compassion to her. So many times I have longed to see her and to show her my love and concern.

More recently, a short while before we left for furlough, John made a quick visit to the tribal area to check some last-minute corrections on Scripture that was ready to be printed. He was surprised one day, as he was going into the town to attend a meeting, to see Turira on the track. In the fading red light of a sun that had already set, he did not at first recognize her. She called his name urgently and then asked after me.

'I want to come and live with Audrey,' she said. 'No one cares for me any more. I am very alone in the world. Take me to live with Audrey.' Even when John explained to her that I was in Brasilia, she was ready to set off there and then. She spoke excitedly, if a little incoherently, pleading with John to take her. Her flushed face confirmed what we had previously heard—that she had been trying to forget her sorrows at the nearby *bolicho*. A wave of sadness swept over John.

He calmed her down and suggested that she come and talk to him on another day. She promised she would, and that was how I was able to hear her voice again—by means of the recorded message she sent me:

'I've come from a long way away, in God's name, to cause my words to be carried to Audrey. I want to talk to her and cause my words to arrive where she is, although she is a long way away. . . .

'I have come back from where I was living far away from here, because I felt very alone, I was homesick for you all. . . . While I was far away I dreamt about Audrey when she went away and disappeared from me. In my dream I found her and was happy again. . . . God cleaned all my heart and because of that it was just as if I was able to talk to her again. Then I prayed and sang. I was able to pray again because God had cleaned my heart: "Come, Lord, and help me so that I can arrive again at Lorena's [Loraine Bridgman's] place. Bless Audrey and John and elder brother [Michael]. Keep them all healthy and cause them to remember me again, even though I am far away. . . . Only You are with me and only You see me, Lord. Really clean my heart, Lord, so that I can go again to John's place and see them all again and sing in my old church again."

'I haven't left God's Word. Every day I say to Him before I sleep (so that I can sleep): "You only are my Saviour. Wherever I am You look after me. You are the only one who can take away my sadness. I am greatly unhappy because I don't have a mother any more, I don't have a father any more, I don't have brothers and sisters any more. But You are up in heaven and You look after me."

'The Lord came down a while ago and stood on the earth. While I lived in that place a long way away He came in a storm. I heard Him in the thunder . . . then He brought me back here. And this is what I say to Him, singing [here she began to sing]:

"When we walk in the garden and when we bring our hearts to God for cleansing, then Jesus will come down.

So we all walked together among the flowers and Jesus descended. I asked Him:

Come to me Jesus, cleanse me,
Jesus, heavenly One.
You are the only One who gives me life,
You are the One who comes to bless me.
Bless me, bless me, O Jesus my Master.
You are the One who has power over everything.
You are the One who is completely holy.
Bless us, bless us and save us from every kind of ill.
Amen, amen, amen, Jesus, amen." '

There was a great deal of repetition in the song, true to Kaiwa style. She was obviously singing extemporaneously.

After the song she described the very violent storm which had impressed her with its significance. She explained that after the storm she couldn't settle any more in that far-off place, and so she had prayed desperately to God that He would bring her back to us and to her friends at the Kaiwa Mission.

When she left John that day she returned to her rootless existence, with no real place to call home. . . .

Where are you now, Turira?
What's happening to you at this moment?
Thank God I can reach you by prayer, wherever you are.

* * *

So many times as I have thought about Turira my mind has gone back to the cameo of the banana palms: 'Where there is true life it is never destroyed.' The palms may be blighted by frost but green shoots will yet appear. Life will triumph over death!

And for you, Turira, a plant blighted by frost, scorched by the sun and trampled on by men, I claim a promise from Isaiah. It is one which you know nothing about as yet, because it has not been translated into your language, but it comforts me greatly when I think of you. Promised to God's people whom He likens to vines, it can surely be appropriated for any who are 'the planting of the Lord':

'I the Lord do keep it; I will water it every moment: lest any hurt it, I will keep it night and day ' (Isaiah 27:3 AV).

15

Benjamin

Julia first came into our lives with Elidio, a short while before the snakebite incident. We have a somewhat faded transparency of them taken about this time, with their two little daughters, Paulina and Lucila. Elidio is holding an old shotgun and standing proudly beside an impressive deerskin, stretched out in the sun to dry. Julia is holding a small green parrot on her finger. I have a feeling that they were interested in selling it to us.

They were just two of a large number of Kaiwa, slightly known to us in those days, and we could never have imagined, then, that our lives would become so inextricably linked.

A few years after Elidio's brush with death, Julia contracted TB. When we returned after our furlough, we found her a very sick woman. We wondered why Elidio, after his own experience at the Mission hospital, had not taken her there. One day he told us.

'Justino won't allow her to go,' he said. 'He is absolutely adamant. He says she is bewitched, and so it's no use taking her to hospital. He has forbidden me to take her. He says she'll die if she goes there. What can I do?'

Justino was in fact only Julia's step-father. Even so, he appeared to have complete jurisdiction in the situation. He was the one who had been shaking rattles and chanting at the door of Elidio's house when John arrived on the day of the snakebite. He had not apparently put up any resistance as the party had left for the hospital on that occasion, but then he doubtless considered snakebite to be different from witchcraft. Sad to say, he was later to die of TB himself, convinced that he too had been bewitched. (He had confided to Julia, 'Unless you discover the witch and undo the witchcraft practised against me, I shall never be healed.')

Elidio was by this time irrevocably involved in the translation programme and helped John whenever possible. During the planting season he suggested that John should go and work at his house. Although this was not so easy for translation work—there was no table and one could only take along a limited number of commentaries—John readily agreed, knowing that it would enable Elidio to work in his fields right up to the moment he arrived and immediately after he left.

On the first day after this arrangement was made, John cycled up to the house to find Julia stretched out on the ground, lying in the hot sun. She did not get up to greet him, and he noticed that her legs and arms were unbelievably thin. From time to time a dry cough racked her body, otherwise she was motionless.

When Elidio appeared, already perspiring from his work in the fields, John was standing there, looking at Julia. They both knew that her condition was very serious and that time was running out.

'Elidio, if we don't get Julia to the hospital right away, she's going to die. Are you still going to listen to Justino when your wife's life is at stake? The decision is yours.'

He hesitated a moment and then said:

'Justino isn't here right now. He left this morning for a week's fishing trip. . . . Yes, I *am* going to take her. Let's go!'

Julia spent six months at the Kaiwa Mission Hospital recovering from TB. This was very hard on Elidio and his children, who now numbered six—two girls and four boys —but they gladly made the sacrifice and frequently visited her, making the long trek to the hospital on foot.

During this time, despite the difficulties, Elidio continued to help John with the translation programme. His help was humbly and faithfully given. We owe much to him for the discovery of words and concepts vital to the clear presentation of Scripture truths.

One day while working on John's first epistle, they came to the well known text, 'God is love' (1 John 4:8). What could be easier than that? But Kaiwa, like many other languages, does not have this kind of construction, and does not express 'love' as an abstract noun. So John described what this meant and asked Elidio how he would express it in his language. He gave

Elidio reading Scripture to his family—
his wife Julia, son Daniel and baby Benjamin.

this very meaningful rendering: 'God, He is the one who has the nature of genuine unconditional love for people.' Often he would show the depth of his understanding by the way he translated certain passages.

Finally Julia was pronounced cured and allowed to return home. And a year later she, who thought she would never again bear a child, had a healthy baby son, right there in her grass-roofed house. As a mark of her gratitude, she asked John to name the baby, and he chose the name Benjamin for this little one who had come, as it were, to celebrate Julia's return from the dead.

Benjamin was very special right from the start, and as soon as he could understand, he learned about Jesus, and as soon as he could talk, he learned to pray and sing. He would never go to sleep at night in his little hammock, made from a strip of blanket, if his father or mother had not prayed with him, and his knowledge of Kaiwa hymns and choruses was very impressive even to his own family.

I shall never forget attending a Sunday afternoon meeting on one occasion, and sitting close to Benjamin on a log in the front row. He was four years old at the time. He sang each hymn and chorus lustily and in perfect tune, and knew all the words by heart. I choked back a few tears as I watched him. They would no doubt have flowed freely had I known what was going to happen.

Whenever Elidio was unable to help John, he would ask Julia to act as his substitute. In this way she was exposed to the Scriptures much more than most Kaiwa women, even other believers. She was an able exponent of her own language and was also very knowledgeable when it came to Kaiwa folklore and culture. She supplied a necessary element in the process of preparing 'God's paper-words' for her people, and her quick unpremeditated reactions would often show up for us an infelicitous phrase or rendering.

She also helped me with the translation and revision of many hymns and choruses, and we would often get into interesting discussions as a result of our research. I came to appreciate her more and more.

One day, after lunch, we were both washing up together. She looked a bit downcast and I asked her why. 'Soon you will be going away [we were going back to Brasilia for the children to go to school] and I won't see you for a while. I'm not happy when you and John aren't here.'

'I too will miss you very much, Julia,' I said. 'I get sick-with-unfulfilled-longing to see you.'

She hung up the tea-towel on its hook and wiped her hands. Then, as she stood looking at them, she slowly drew a ring from her finger and handed it to me. It had been made from the black shell of a nut, cut into sections. Each section made a ring. The outside was polished until it shone. She had made this one herself. 'Put it on, Audrey,' she said, 'and whenever you look at it, remember to pray for me. Pray that I will go on trusting Jesus whatever may happen.' Did she know how much she would need my prayers?

* * *

We were not there when it happened. I had been to collect our mail in Brasilia one afternoon, when I noticed a letter from Kaiwa-land. I opened it first, and took out two closely written sheets. They were from Elidio and Julia. I was not at all prepared for what they contained. As it happened I read Elidio's first, partly because it is not always easy in a Kaiwa letter to tell who it is from. Sometimes the information 'I, Elidio, am sending my paper-words' does not come at the very beginning, nor at the very end.

When John came in and looked at me, my face—drained of all colour—told him something was wrong. 'I can't believe it,' I said. 'It's Benjamin . . . he's died. Look, here it says: "And so he died, Benjamin." Read it, John. Perhaps I have misunderstood it.'

But I had not misunderstood it. It was all described in great detail, from the first day when he felt the terrible stomach pains, to the last day when even the most skilled doctors in the town's hospital had not been able to save him. And Benjamin himself, just five years old, after praying in front of the doctors, had said: 'I know I am not going to get better.'

Julia wrote: 'My older-sister, Audrey—I am not happy any more. My innermost is squeezed. Pray for me. Pray for all of us. We put Benjamin into our Great Chief's hands, and He took him. Even so we still trust Him.

'We always pray for you. When are you coming back to us? Keep on praying for us.

'And now my words are finished.'

The testimony of this Christian Kaiwa couple will never be forgotten by the doctors involved in the case. With Benjamin's intestine so badly blocked, the only hope—and it was a slender one—was to attempt to remove a section of the bowel. The doctor, a sympathetic man although not a believer, warned Elidio that a high percentage of patients do not survive the operation.

'Well, doctor,' Elidio said, 'I want you to know that we have put our son's life into the hands of God. We know you are a skilled doctor and will do your best. If Benjamin doesn't get better, we will not blame you. We will accept it as the will of God.'

* * *

When we returned to them, there was an air of sadness about Julia. 'My heart is still crushed, and I do not eat,' she said. 'So many things remind me of Benjamin, especially some of the hymns, and I loved him so very much. But I have come to understand it all a little. Jesus also loved Benjamin, and He saw that Benjamin loved Him, too . . . and He just wanted to have him always near Him. That's all.'

Having observed the lives of the Kaiwa from close quarters for many years, and having seen their suffering, their total lack of material comfort, and their familiarity with death, both John and I had almost taken it for granted that God would not expect them to suffer as Christians as well. By this assumption we showed that we had not fully understood the purpose and the necessity of suffering in the Christian life.

God's aim is to produce mature Kaiwa Christians, whose faith has stood the test, so that they will be able to take their place as 'overcomers' along with those of all the other nations, around the Great White Throne. He does not deny them this glory. He is working to this end. 'Indeed all who desire to live a godly life in Christ Jesus will be persecuted' (2 Timothy 3:12 RSV). It is promised in Scripture. So we should not have been surprised at what followed: subtle persecutions of various kinds, beatings, imprisonments and slander. The list reads almost like Paul's accomplishments, or the sufferings of the 'men of faith' in Hebrews. If Jesus had not been suffering along with them, we would have marvelled that He could have allowed it.

On one of our last visits, we were at the Kaiwa Mission. As all our members had received an official order to withdraw from Indian land, we were unable to visit the Kaiwa in their own homes. But in spite of this, they came to us, and we would have almost as many Indians in the house as in the old days.

Some mornings our verandah filled right up. After catching up on all the news, I would leave an ample supply of National Geographics for them to peruse, so that I could attend to some of the household chores.

They loved the pictures of wildlife, and I learned a lot of vocabulary as I listened to them. Sometimes it was quite like a pantomime out there. It only took one or two funny comments to have everyone roaring with laughter. Listening to it, I thought it was better than any television show. If I wasn't there to translate the captions, they would try to interpret some of the magazine pictures in terms of their own culture—with bizarre results. I loved to hear them.

One day there happened to be a Bible storybook among the magazines. Someone began looking at it and asking questions. I was in the kitchen at the time, making tea for my visitors. And then I heard Julia, who was actually waiting to work with me, begin to explain what the pictures were all about. The whole group was silent and listened, and I was amazed at her understanding, as she unfolded to them God's plan in creation and salvation. Her hours at the translation desk had not been wasted.

Gradually the group dwindled, and Julia and I went off to a quiet place to work. I was preparing some messages that I had been asked to record for women's meetings at Fern Village and Alligator Water down in the south. Having prayed about it, I felt I should do one on 'forgiveness' and another on 'gossip'. I wanted to find just the right way of putting into Kaiwa what I was trying to say.

We started by discussing the subject and it was just like

opening a floodgate. The Holy Spirit knew that this was something that was bothering Julia a great deal, and that she needed to be able to talk about it. She told me some of the things that had been happening in the area where she lived, and about the lies that had been spread around about herself and members of her family.

'It makes me very angry,' she said. 'What does God's Word have to say about this sort of thing?'

So we looked up various Scripture passages to find out what Jesus said:

'But I say unto you, Love your enemies, bless them that curse you, do good to them that hate you, and pray for them which despitefully use you, and persecute you' (Matthew 5:44 AV).

' "How many times do I have to forgive. . . .? Seven times?" "No, not seven times," answered Jesus, "but seventy times seven" ' (Matthew 18:21–22 GNB).

And I told Julia of some recent experiences of my own that had tested this principle to its utmost limit:

'I too, Julia, find it very hard to forgive, but God says if I don't, then He will not forgive me. Do you remember what it says in the Lord's Prayer? So I'll pray for you, and you must pray for me, that together we may become more like Jesus.' We closed our eyes. Her prayer for me, so eloquently expressed, has been and is being answered, because it came right from the heart of God.

And this is where my role as a missionary reaches its zenith —when I can share my faith and experience with a Kaiwa woman as she shares hers with me. And some of the question-marks that have hung over the bitter experiences of my life have been removed as I have seen their relevance to the experiences of my Kaiwa sisters. This is how we are drawn together; this is how people from entirely different cultures can grow together in that unity that was the heart-yearning of Jesus when He prayed, 'That they may all be *one*. . . even as we are one' (John 17:21–22 AV).

* * *

So here, for the time being anyway, is the last of my cameos. It is, in a way, the one that makes sense of all the others, for this sharing, this bearing of each other's burdens, is a crowning glory. Each cameo has been different, each picture a reminder of something Jesus had to do in me. I'm glad He cared enough to carve them and leave them with me so that I couldn't forget.

And what He has done for me He is doing in all corners of the tribe for individual Kaiwas, who have responded to Him. His word has not returned to Him void. It has accomplished His purposes. Through the devoted service of Brazilian Christians in the Kaiwa Mission, through other Wycliffe members who are or have been involved with the Kaiwa people, through those who have served faithfully through their gifts and prayers, as well as through me—who am the least of these —God reaches out to a forgotten people and brings them into His family. They also have the honour of bearing the family likeness.

And through it all I see that He is very concerned with carving. I see that I too am being carved. It is His purpose that I should bear the Father's image, engraved upon the unique material that is *me*. However costly the process, this above all things has become my desire.

> I find crosses Christ's carved work that He marketh out for us, and that with crosses He figureth and portrayeth us to His own image, cutting away pieces of our ill and corruption. Lord, cut, Lord carve, Lord wound, Lord do anything that may perfect Thy Father's image in us, and make us meet for glory.
>
> Samuel Rutherford, *The Loveliness of Christ.*

I have no doubt that he is at work on my cameo. There is much more to be done yet, but when it is finished, He will present it to His Father, unique and faultless—another example of His eternal workmanship.

Onyx
Rich in colour
Smooth as glass
Oval
Let no scratch
Mar its natural beauty.

Who but He who sees
Within its ivory layer
A portrait rare
Would dare
To carve?

Long years
And then
Last shaving smoothed away
He stands back
Viewing
That delicate creation
Onyx pale on
Onyx richly coloured
Cameo
Most intricately bevelled
And gazing
From blistered fingers
To the finished gem
Will He not then
Announce
His pleasure?

Glossary and Pronunciation Guide

In Kaiwa, stress generally falls on the final syllable. The stressed syllabale will be capitalized in the words that follow.

x is pronounced as 'sh'.

y is a central vowel similar to the unstressed *a* in such phrases as 'have *a* go' and 'rent *a* house', or like *er* (British English) in words such as 'butt*er*', 'moth*er*' etc. The symbol used here to avoid confusion with the vowel 'a' will be 'er' ('ER' if stressed).

Kaiwa—kighWAH (-igh as in 'high').

Tatu'y—tatoo'ER—Armadillo Water.

Rosinha—hoZEEnya—one of our first language helpers.

Panambi—panamBEE—Butterfly Village.

charrete—shaHETchi—two-wheeled, horse-drawn cart.

urucu—oorooKOO—large bush with red seeds in prickly pods.

Chikinho—shiKEEnyoo—leading witchdoctor at Butterfly Village.

kangwi—kangWEE—corn-liquor.

Elidio—iLEEjoo—young Kaiwa man bitten by a snake.

Loide Andrade—LOYji anDRAHji—one of the directors of the Kaiwa Mission. Her husband, Orlando, also a director, is Pastor of the Mission church.

tumbyky—toomberKER—marrow-like vegetable.

bolicho—boLEEshoo—small wayside store selling basic necessities and also *pinga*, cheap gin.

Turira—tooREEra—a Kaiwa woman (see chapter 14). Her name was probably *Turilha* when originally given.

Aurora—owRORa—Turira's daughter. Her name means 'Dawn'.

Osirio—orSEErioo—Turira's first husband.